I0824386

ANOTHER KIND OF FREEDOM

BOOKS BY PEMA CHÖDRÖN

Awakening Loving-Kindness
Becoming Bodhisattvas
Comfortable with Uncertainty
The Compassion Book
How We Live Is How We Die
Living Beautifully
The Places That Scare You
The Pocket Pema Chödrön
Practicing Peace
Start Where You Are
Taking the Leap
Welcoming the Unwelcome
When Things Fall Apart
The Wisdom of No Escape

ANOTHER KIND OF FREEDOM

A student's commentary on
The Myth of Freedom and the Way of Meditation
by Chögyam Trungpa

PEMA CHÖDRÖN

SHAMBHALA

Shambhala Publications, Inc.
2129 13th Street
Boulder, Colorado 80302
www.shambhala.com

Cover art: KanitChurem/Adobe Stock
Cover design: Daniel Urban-Brown
Interior design: Kate E. White

9 8 7 6 5 4 3 2 1

First Edition
Printed in the United States of America

Shambhala Publications makes every effort to print on acid-free, recycled paper. Shambhala Publications is distributed worldwide by Penguin Random House, Inc., and its subsidiaries.

Library of Congress Cataloging-in-Publication Data
Names: Chödrön, Pema author
Title: Another kind of freedom: A student's commentary on *The Myth of Freedom and the Way of Meditation* by Chögyam Trungpa; commentary by Pema Chödrön.
Description: Boulder: Shambhala Publications, 2026. | Material from *The Myth of Freedom* by Chögyam Trungpa (Shambhala, 1976 — page 4. |
Identifiers: LCCN 2025024760 | ISBN 9781645473268 hardback
Subjects: LCSH: Spiritual life—Buddhism | Meditation—Buddhism | Buddhism—Doctrines | Trungpa, Chögyam, 1939–1987. The Myth of Freedom and the Way of Meditation.
Classification: LCC BQ7805 .C4843 2026
LC record available at https://lccn.loc.gov/2025024760

The authorized representative in the EU for product safety and compliance is eucomply OÜ, Pärnu mnt 139b-14, 11317 Tallinn, Estonia, hello@eucompliancepartner.com.

This book is dedicated with heartfelt devotion
and gratitude to my root teacher
Chökyi Gyatso
Ocean of Dharma
The Vidyhadara Chögyam Trungpa Rinpoche

CONTENTS

SEVEN

Devotion

EIGHT

Tantra

INTRODUCTION

When I first encountered the Buddhist teachings in the early 1970s, there were not many teachers who taught in a voice that Western students could connect with in a personal way. The only ones I came across were the Zen master Shunryu Suzuki Roshi, who started San Francisco Zen Center, and my root teacher Chögyam Trungpa Rinpoche. Both were tremendously curious about the West, and both had a passion for teaching Western students.

For me, it was amazing to read Suzuki Roshi's *Zen Mind, Beginner's Mind* and Trungpa Rinpoche's books *Cutting Through Spiritual Materialism* and *The Myth of Freedom and the Way of Meditation* (which I will refer to as *The Myth of Freedom* throughout this book). These books didn't feel like Buddhist philosophy at all. They felt like advice for everyday life and neuroses—particularly everyday neuroses, which there were plenty of.

We're often drawn to a spiritual path because we are hurting and looking for answers. So it's difficult when the teachings you hear are so philosophical that you can't figure out how they connect with your everyday pain and confusion—with the fact that you blow up all the time, or the fact that you have low self-esteem, or whatever your particular brand of suffering is. The directness and relevance of Rinpoche's teachings were what really bowled me over, and they bowled over many other people as well.

The Myth of Freedom is an edited compilation drawn from public talks that Rinpoche gave in various places during the early 1970s. In 2007, I felt inspired to share my love of this book and to convey to a live audience how Rinpoche's teachings have helped me. So it came to pass that for six weeks, in Berkeley, California, I gave the teachings that you'll find in this book.

Whenever I read *The Myth of Freedom*, I'm surprised to rediscover how much this book has influenced me. If you're familiar with any of my teachings, you'll probably read something Rinpoche says here, and you'll think, "That's what Pema always says"—as if I was the one who made it up! Chögyam Trungpa Rinpoche's words have become part of my bloodstream, so much so that I may not always realize when I'm borrowing from him. They have inspired my deep passion for this spiritual path, a passion I hope to share with you.

WHAT I MEAN BY ANOTHER KIND OF FREEDOM

As you read this book, keep in mind that Rinpoche is continually giving us the instructions for how to experience what he calls **an ultimate and fundamental sense of freedom**. He helps us glimpse what this ultimate freedom actually feels like—what it is experientially—and he teaches us what gets in the way of connecting with it.

The freedom that most of us cherish is temporary and fleeting. It may come as a gift that lasts for a while but ultimately doesn't address our fundamental dissatisfaction, our underlying anxiety. I once received a letter from a man who was released from prison after spending twenty years incarcerated for a crime he didn't commit. During those two decades, he naturally yearned for freedom: to be able to walk out his door whenever he wanted, to see and smell the ocean, to take long walks in the hills, to look up at the stars and moon at night. "Now," he wrote, "it's two years later, and I easily do all these things, but somehow I'm still an unhappy man." The joy of his freedom was short-lived, and now he sought to address his far deeper dissatisfaction, his fundamental discontent. He asked me if I thought that meditation might help him, and if the Buddhist teachings might have anything to offer. I responded that they were very likely just what he was looking for.

I think the kind of freedom he felt when he left prison was what Rinpoche calls "the myth of freedom." No matter how wonderful it is, it's still fleeting. What Rinpoche addresses in his book, and what I address in my commentary, presents "another kind of freedom," the freedom that liberates us from the very causes of suffering. This kind of freedom isn't swayed by external circumstances. It's what we feel when we settle down with life as it is, when we give in to being right on the spot, when we learn to make friends with ourselves at all times and in all situations.

ABOUT THE ORGANIZATION OF THIS BOOK

The Myth of Freedom is composed of eight chapters, each divided into several sections. In my 2007 Berkeley talks, I stayed as close as I could to the content and structure of the original. Since it was impractical to read through Rinpoche's entire book in the course of six talks, I selected certain parts to read aloud and comment on, doing my best to choose the material that went most directly to the essence of Rinpoche's teachings.

In this book version, I've clarified—and in certain areas, expanded on—my original presentation. Each chapter or section title in my commentary is the same as that of its corresponding part in *The Myth of Freedom.* It would enhance your experience to read each section of Rinpoche's book before reading what I have to say about it. I've put direct quotes from *The Myth of Freedom* in bold to differentiate them from quotes from other sources.

Finally, *Rinpoche* is an honorific term in Tibetan that literally means "Precious One" and is generally used for someone who has been identified as the rebirth of a previous important teacher. In this book, the name Rinpoche, when used alone, will always refer to Chögyam Trungpa Rinpoche. When I mention or quote other Rinpoches, I will give more of their name to avoid ambiguity.

BODHICHITTA ASPIRATION

Before getting into the content of *The Myth of Freedom,* let's do what I always do at the beginning of each book or teaching I give—establish a clear motivation. Why in the world am I giving this teaching, and why in the world are you reading or listening to it? There could be any number of reasons, but in the mahayana Buddhist tradition to which I belong, there is one overarching intention, known as *bodhichitta*—the heartfelt longing to awaken in order to be of benefit to others.

Bodhichitta is a vast aspiration, but it starts with yourself. In the simplest and humblest words, you can say, "As a result of reading these teachings, contemplating them, discussing them with others, and so on, may I become a saner person. May I become less caught up, hysterical, and confused. May I awaken my heart and mind so that I can be of some benefit to the immense suffering that we see all over the earth today. May I at least be saner and more helpful with the people in my daily life—my family, my coworkers, the people I meet in the store."

We can make such aspirations at the beginning of not only teachings but any activity. We can also state this intention in more formal and traditional terms, such as by reciting the following lines, which come from an aspiration called the Four Limitless Ones:

> May all sentient beings enjoy happiness and
> the root of happiness.
> May they be free from suffering and the root
> of suffering.

It may seem mechanical to use traditional words and language, but they can help us give voice to our higher intention: that whatever we do will add up to benefiting ourselves and others in the greatest possible way. This is the motivation that Rinpoche and all my other teachers have carried with them in all activities throughout their lives.

Enlightenment, as taught in Buddhism, refers to a state of unconditional well-being and freedom from suffering. We wish to become enlightened, not only for ourselves but in order to help everyone else attain this state. But our vast intention starts with simply becoming saner people. As we become less neurotic, we become better equipped to help others get free from their own suffering. To the degree that our confusion lessens, to that degree we can help others lessen their own confusion. We can become supremely beneficial to ourselves and others at the same time.

ONE

THE MYTH OF FREEDOM

FANTASY AND REALITY

THE FIRST CHAPTER of *The Myth of Freedom* has four sections: "Fantasy and Reality," "Disappointment," "Suffering," and "Egolessness."

In the course of a prolific teaching career that spanned over two decades, Chögyam Trungpa Rinpoche gave more than two thousand talks to public and private audiences. These have resulted in over forty books. His penetrating, accessible language covered almost the entire range of the Buddhist teachings. But throughout this outpouring of dharma, a few key themes flowed continually like a river through Rinpoche's teachings.

One of these themes is perhaps the simplest theme possible. As he says here in "Fantasy and Reality," **The basic practice is to be present, right here.**

Be present. Be right here. This was one of his foremost messages. Be just where you are—wherever you are, whoever you are, whatever is happening, fully present, on the spot, without seeking exits, alternatives, or sidetracks.

This universally important instruction was especially appropriate for Rinpoche's early students, who were mostly hippies, myself included. Many of us sought transcendent experiences. Consciously or unconsciously, we went into spirituality to leave this messy world behind. We hoped to become cleaned-up, more spiritual versions of ourselves. We hoped our personalities would get smoothed over and we'd turn into serene people who never got triggered—who were very *together*. This produced a lot of people who appeared calm but were oozing with emotional reactivity.

The audience today appears tamer, but I don't think we're quite free of that tendency. The underlying wish to get away from the unpleasantness of life is a strong motivating force for most sentient beings.

Rinpoche's teachings emphasized working with what was on our plate—our current circumstances, our struggles, our emotional turmoil. What's on your plate is the working basis for your spiritual practice, not something better later. In the most basic terms, this comes down to being present—fully and utterly present.

"Fantasy and Reality" points directly to this basic theme. "Fantasy" refers to wishing you were somewhere else, and "reality" refers to being right where you are. When we fantasize about being somewhere else, we're not appreciating where we are.

Rinpoche encouraged us not to complain about our karma. He taught us that all our experience, from what happened this morning to our overall life situation, is the result of karma—more commonly known as "we reap what we sow" or "what goes around comes around." In the past, you have sown a variety of karmic seeds, helpful ones and unhelpful ones. Now these seeds are ripening as your current experience.

Thinking that your current situation is somebody else's fault is futile. But blaming yourself and thinking that you're therefore a bad person is even more futile. Westerners have a strong tendency to take a punishment view of karma and all too frequently to blame ourselves whenever unwanted circumstances arrive.

Rinpoche encouraged us to abandon these counterproductive approaches. It is far more helpful to think, "The past got me to this point, but the future is wide open. How I relate to this moment—what I do right now—will determine what happens next, in the short term and in the long term." Instead of assigning blame, we can gradually free ourselves from our repetitive karmic patterns. Instead of going the habitual route by digging the hole even deeper, we can become a bit saner, day after day. The way to become fully sane is to train in being right here. And the key method for that training is meditation.

Meditation is our practice for training in just being here with whatever is happening—pleasant, unpleasant, or neutral. Instead of perpetuating our fantasy, meditation connects us with reality.* Thus the opening sentence of "Fantasy and Reality": **If we are to plant the complete Buddhist teachings in American soil, we must first understand the fundamental principles of Buddhism and work through its basic meditation practices.**

Before saying more about meditation, Rinpoche warns us of certain pitfalls that might get in the way of our practice bearing fruit: **Many people respond to Buddhism as if it were a new cult which might save them, which might enable them to deal with the world in the manner of picking flowers in a beautiful garden. But if we wish to pick flowers from a tree, we must first cultivate the roots and**

* See the appendix for basic instructions on sitting meditation.

trunk, which means that we must work with our fears, frustrations, disappointments, and irritations, the painful aspects of life.

Rather than reject what's challenging, embarrassing, or unpleasant, he encouraged us to "lean into the sharp points." He repeated this message over and over again, knowing that it went against the human tendency to use spirituality to skip over what is painful.

Some of the material that went into *The Myth of Freedom* came from a seminar titled "Buddhadharma without Credentials," which Rinpoche taught in New York City in 1973. The title referred to practicing Buddhism without it feeding your ego. With the credential approach, instead of weakening your self-absorption, you become more self-centered. You build up your ego by joining the club of Buddhism. Maybe you even brag. You feel so proud to be doing this special thing with this outrageous Tibetan lama. It's a feather in your cap, a credential.

Rinpoche knew this me-centric attitude was counterproductive, and he was very straightforward about pointing that out. This is how he began that seminar:

> The subject we're going to discuss is buddhadharma without credentials. For the past three years, since I've been in this country, I've been repeating the same things again and again and again in order to emphasize what needs to be developed and what dangers should be watched for on the spiritual path. I personally feel committed to teaching, needless to say. It's my life, it's my karma, and because of that I feel extremely committed to relating to the people of this continent. Presenting the

> teachings faithfully is possibly boring, painful, and not particularly glamorous. But from my point of view, it is for the benefit of future generations.

In the same talk, Rinpoche says that "it seems to be the destined karmic flow that Buddhism is obviously going to come to America, and America is going to become the home of Buddhism. Sooner or later that is going to happen. So if we are going to be instrumental in bringing that about, we should disregard the advertisement aspect of it."

He warns against "the Madison Avenue style with all the gimmicks and seductive highlights and promises." When I read that now I think about the advertisements you see whenever you pick up any spiritual magazine. You get the meditation cushion, you get the leotard. You get the books, and you listen to the recordings. But maybe it's just a new thrill, a new fad, a new credential.

Not only that, but it also comes with a promise—that as a result of this, you will improve and be happy. It's interesting because the bodhichitta aspiration prayer *does* say, "May all sentient beings enjoy happiness." But the subtle point is that we add "and the root of happiness." We can only achieve happiness by discovering its true causes. Those causes, you won't be surprised to hear from a spiritual teacher, are not outer material possessions. When Rinpoche discusses the causes of happiness in *The Myth of Freedom*, they have more to do with how we work internally with what's unfolding in our lives than with fixing outer circumstances. In other words, our happiness depends on how we work with our reactions to the outer circumstances, how we work with our mind and emotions.

If we're going to really do this, Rinpoche said, we have to give up what he called "spiritual materialism." In the New York seminar, he said, "We could work on a much more fundamental, basic, and honest level. Therefore, I have been presenting the idea of spiritual materialism."

Rinpoche talks about spiritual materialism in depth in his book *Cutting Through Spiritual Materialism*, and I recommend that you read it to deepen your understanding. Basically it's another way of talking about credentials. You could even call it buddhadharma *with* credentials—using the teachings and the practices to build up our ego. If the spiritual path is about ventilating our habitual patterns and neurotic ways, then we don't want to compound the problem by adding a *spiritual* neurosis—a spiritual layer of confusion.

Self-centeredness comes in many forms. For instance, you're talking to someone, and you're engaged, open, and present—you're fully with them. Then, out of nowhere, an old habitual pattern kicks in. You didn't mean to think this, but the thought comes: "Did I say something stupid?" Or "I wonder if I'm looking unattractive." Basically it comes down to "What do they think of me?" All of a sudden, you've split in two, and you're not hearing anything they're saying. The other person is almost not there anymore. It's all about you.

This sense of "all about me" has great power over us. However, the point isn't to get rid of ego. The point is to relate to it so honestly that it loses its power over us. If we use meditation practice and the teachings of Buddhism to acquire a new identity as a Buddhist or a meditator, then we are engaging in spiritual materialism. In those days, Rinpoche saw spiritual materialism everywhere, and he presented the simplest way of working with it: "Just relate to yourself as you are right now and accept that." Relating to yourself as you are is so unglamorous that it tends to cut through spiritual materialism. Most of the time, accepting ourselves as we are is not what we want to do.

In the second paragraph of "Fantasy and Reality," Rinpoche says that **according to the Buddha, we must begin by seeing the experience of life as it is.** We often feel like we want to escape because we don't like how we're feeling. As my teenage granddaughter says, "I don't want to be here." We have our own ways of not being here, from addictions to talking to ourselves. Instead, it would be a lot more helpful, and certainly more kind, to encourage ourselves to get curious about the experience of life as it is when we slow down and decide to stop running.

Over the years, I've come to realize what we lose by not staying present with what's happening, and by exiting in our old, familiar ways. Only when we stay present with what's happening does the space open up for us to relax and appreciate ourselves and our world. Rinpoche says that **all sects and schools of Buddhism agree that we must begin by facing the reality of our living situations. We cannot begin by dreaming. That would only be a temporary escape; real escape is impossible.**

From the very beginning, Rinpoche was pointing his students toward a down-to-earth, direct contact with reality. He would teach this way to everyone, old-timers and newcomers alike, talking about not exiting and no sidetracks. He used this kind of language over and over. And what I now understand is that there's nothing more profound.

Rinpoche goes on to talk about the purpose of meditation. **In Buddhism,** he says, **we express our willingness**

to be realistic through the practice of meditation. That's what the practice of meditation is: willingness to be realistic, willingness to stay present and make friends with all parts of ourselves—with our wisdom and our confusion, our neuroses and our sanity. As he says later in the section, **It is an attitude of fundamental acceptance of oneself while still retaining critical intelligence.**

He compares our neuroses to manure: **Like manure, we do not throw our neuroses away, but we spread them on our garden; they become part of our richness.** (His first book, *Meditation in Action*, has a whole chapter on this topic: "The Manure of Experience and the Field of Bodhi.") His approach to meditation is that it's not about becoming a better person, about smoothing things out. Instead, you have to start by creating the space so you can see who you are and make friends with that.

I remember once asking Rinpoche at a public talk, "Rinpoche, you always talk about making friends with ourselves, but it seems to me that the more I see what I do, the more proof I get of how messed up I am." He answered, "Go more deeply into that feeling of messed up and make friends with that."

In fact, Rinpoche emphasized letting your neuroses come to the surface. You can imagine that a lot of his audience dropped away fast: "You want me to do a meditation practice that will bring the neurosis to the surface instead of getting rid of it? It sounds like the result of this is that I'll be neurotic forever."

Rinpoche taught that our neuroses would only dwindle if we accepted ourselves and stopped struggling, if we didn't go to war with ourselves, if we didn't think, "I have to get rid of that embarrassing, hateful part of myself." He encouraged us to value our neurosis. We have to really know it—its smell, its taste, and its texture. On the other hand, appreciating the richness of our neurosis doesn't mean acting it out. We don't repress it, and we don't act it out. We stay fully present. We stay right in the middle.

Returning to our recurring theme, Rinpoche says, **The basic practice is to be present, right here.** That's what we're doing each time we come back to our breath in meditation. We just come back to right here. You can practice this all the time, not only in formal meditation. Whatever you're doing, notice when your mind wanders off and simply come back. This is how we can work with our distracted mind—just come back.

I used to give the instruction to "stay." But I often got the feedback that it's not so much about learning to stay as it is about learning to come back. That is where most of us are. We can't stay all the time, but we can keep coming back, over and over again.

Rinpoche then talks about the meditation practice known as *shamatha*, which is a Sanskrit word meaning "calm abiding" or "the development of peace." **With this practice,** he says, **we begin to tread the hinayana, or narrow, path.**

Rinpoche taught us in the way he was trained, according to the three vehicles, or *yanas*, of hinayana, mahayana, and vajrayana. *Hinayana* literally means "lesser vehicle," so the word can seem to imply, "You do this now and then later you get on to the real stuff." For this reason, many people prefer to call it the "foundation yana." But interestingly, the most advanced vajrayana teachings—the teachings of Mahamudra and Dzogchen—teach much of what Rinpoche presented right from the beginning as the so-called hinayana path. In fact, in Rinpoche's presentation, it can sometimes be hard to distinguish what yana you're on because he says some of the same things in all three levels: Be present, don't exit, open to life as it is.

He refers to the hinayana as **a disciplined path without sidetracks** and adds that **the simplicity of narrowness also brings an open attitude toward life situations, because we realize that there is no escape of any kind and give in to being right on the spot**.

In 1976, he gave an interview in *The Laughing Man* magazine that was titled "Things Get Very Clear When You're Cornered." That image has made a lasting impression on me. You've painted yourself into the corner and you literally can't get away—and then everything gets extraordinarily clear. When there's nowhere to run, you stop looking for alternatives and deal with what's in front of you. This is what he means by **the simplicity of narrowness**.

If you've ever had a life crisis where the rug was pulled out so thoroughly that you couldn't escape no matter how hard you tried, then you know what he means. You think, "Nobody in their right mind would go through this voluntarily." But on the other hand, you realize that when you can't escape and have to be completely present, it's a life changer.

You have to **give in to being right on the spot**. This is hard to do but somehow easy to understand. But then he goes into a related theme that's not so easy to understand. There's something more than just relating to life directly, though that is powerful and important. There's something more than not feeding your habitual tendencies to run away. He says that **becoming more clearly aware of emotions and life situa-**

tions and the space in which they occur might open us to a still more panoramic awareness. This is like a person blind from birth who gains their sight and experiences all the color and vastness that has been here all along.

Of course, you can only really understand what he means by "panoramic awareness" if you experience it. The way to experience it is to be present, and the way to train in being present is to meditate. This is how things can begin to open up and you can gain a wider perspective.

I often encourage people to do this simple practice: As you go about your day, pause every once in a while, look out, and take three conscious breaths. Most of the time, we go through our days caught up in a bubble of thoughts. With this practice, we interrupt the momentum of being caught up for the duration of three conscious breaths. We pause. We look out, and there's the world. Suddenly we have a wider perspective, a more panoramic awareness.

Even without trying, we experience brief moments like these, moments where our mind stops and we see things clearly—moments of awe, wonder, shock, or surprise. In times of tremendous shock, this can happen for an extended period. It seems that time slows down and the space opens up, but all that's happening is we're connecting with the natural openness that's been here all along.

I felt like Rinpoche held nothing back. He drew from his vast knowledge of the Buddhist teachings using whatever he thought would get through to us and help us to wake up. He spoke as if we would all know what he was talking about (even today I'm not always sure what he was talking about), and somehow this communicated right to the heart. He was always looking for ways to lead us beyond spiritual materialism, beyond avoiding life as it is. He was innovative and creative in presenting the message that whatever you've got, that is your spiritual path.

"Fantasy and Reality" concludes with this down-to-earth statement: **The whole approach of Buddhism is to develop transcendental common sense, seeing things as they are, without magnifying what is or dreaming about what we would like to be.**

DISAPPOINTMENT

THIS SECTION continues many of the same ideas. Rinpoche repeats the theme of not using the spiritual path as a credential. **As long as one's approach to spirituality is based upon enriching ego,** he says, **then it is spiritual materialism.** Instead of using drugs, alcohol, sex, shopping, or anything else, you use spirituality to avoid pain—the pain of your living situation or the pain of being who you are. This is the essence of spiritual materialism. As Oprah Winfrey once said, "If you're seeking continual pleasure and always trying to avoid pain, you're on the wrong planet."

Rinpoche didn't want people wasting their time trying to achieve a life with no ups and downs. He wanted Buddhism to be like good medicine for the people in our culture. So he took things that normally are thought of as bad news—for example, disappointment and boredom—and showed how they could be a big help on one's spiritual path.

In this section, he connects disappointment with expectation or wishful thinking: **We expect the teachings to solve all our problems; we expect to be provided with magical means to deal with our depressions, our aggressions, our sexual hangups. But to our surprise we begin to realize that this is not going to happen. It is very disappointing to realize that we must work on ourselves and our suffering rather**

than depend upon a savior or the magical power of yogic techniques. It is disappointing to realize that we have to give up our expectations rather than build on the basis of our preconceptions.

When you're disappointed, things didn't go the way you expected, the way they were supposed to. As long as you have the expectation that you can get things to work out your way, you'll be disappointed. Sometimes they do, sometimes they don't; that's the reality. A better approach is to do things wholeheartedly but leave the future open-ended. You know what you want, but you're realistic. Outcomes are unpredictable.

Disappointment, however, can also lead to an aha moment: "Why am I so upset? I was holding on to some expectation of things going a certain way. That's why I'm so upset." You begin to see disappointment differently, as something that could help you wake up. Rinpoche appreciated disappointment because, as he says, it is **without the ambition of the ego**. The pain of disappointment pops the bubble of ego very effectively. Instead of building up your ego, it makes you feel more vulnerable. This of course is just what many of us don't want. When we feel even the hint of vulnerability, we armor ourselves. But it doesn't have to be that way.

My experience with disappointment is that when you're really let down and hurting, the teachings don't change your emotional reaction. Whether it's a small thing, like the restaurant being closed, or a major thing, like being betrayed in a relationship, the teachings don't prevent you from having that disappointed feeling. This is an important point. Your emotional reaction may not change, but your response to that reaction changes. In my life, I don't try to make everything okay. That would be my knee-jerk response. Instead I try to move closer to the feeling of disappointment and let it pierce me to the heart.

Recently something happened where I totally lost it and exploded in anger. This was quite unexpected and painful—after *all* these years of practice. What do I do with my embarrassment and the pain of having hurt somebody? I blew it; I made myself suffer, and I made someone else suffer. How can I stay present with those feelings so that I don't create further pain by trying to get away from what just happened? These are the kinds of questions I ask myself. The disappointment doesn't change; what changes is how I respond. I can get swept up in the emotional turmoil, or I can interrupt the momentum and not escalate. As Rinpoche would say, "We're given choices every moment of our life to wake up further or go further to sleep." Do I make matters worse, or do I taste the rawness of what I'm feeling and lean in?

As the ambition of ego dwindles, Rinpoche says we become like a "grain of sand": **We fall down and down and down, until we touch the ground, until we relate with the basic sanity of earth. We become the lowest of the low, the smallest of the small, a grain of sand, perfectly simple, no expectations. When we are grounded, there is no room for dreaming or frivolous impulse, so our practice at last becomes workable.**

Becoming a grain of sand has nothing to do with being pitiful or self-denigrating. It's the experience of getting out of your own way and becoming more receptive to the world: **If you are a grain of sand, the rest of the universe, all the space, all the room is yours, because you obstruct nothing, overcrowd nothing, possess nothing. There is tremendous openness.**

This is the opposite of the big-deal attitude he describes so humorously in "Buddhadharma without Credentials":

> If I practice more, will I get credentials, so that I will be entitled to put "Buddha" at the end of my name? Maybe I could at least have "Arhat" or "Bodhisattva" at the end of my name: Jack Parsons, the Bodhisattva; Daniel Smith, the Arhat. The obvious answer to such notions is that the spiritual path is not divided in terms of grades.

In the previous section, I described a conversation where you're connecting with someone and then you suddenly retreat into yourself. You split off, and "me" becomes more important than the other person. When you catch yourself doing that, try becoming a grain of sand. That is to say, stop talking to yourself and open further to the other person. Instead of shaming yourself or making it a big deal, you simply open to the other person. You get out of the way and listen. You allow for curiosity and appreciation.

SUFFERING

IN "BUDDHADHARMA without Credentials," Rinpoche cautions us against being "smooth-oriented" and believing in "some kind of basic harmony." He says that the big area of life that's usually not acknowledged on the spiritual path is the everyday chaos, the everyday "eruption of tremendous energy." Our spiritual journey has to consider how life really is: bitter and sweet, rough and smooth. As he liked to say, "There is no cure for hot and cold."

Our preference for harmony gives us a lopsided view of life, a view that always brings dissatisfaction. Rinpoche's declaration that "chaos is good news" definitely turns our habitual responses upside down. As a student in those days, I was thrilled by statements like this. But I can tell you that it's a long way from being thrilled to actually being able to live in this way.

When I read this section on suffering, Rinpoche's description of our preference for smoothness sounds uncomfortably familiar: **As we grow older,** he writes, **in one way or another we begin to ask, "What is the meaning of life?"** He goes through some potential responses: **We should discover wisdom and share it with others. Or we should create a better political order, reinforcing democracy so that all people are equal and everyone has a right to do whatever they**

want within the limits of mutual responsibility. Perhaps we should raise the level of our civilization to the highest point so that our world becomes a fantastic place, a seat of wisdom, of enlightenment, of learning . . . There should be plenty to eat, pleasant houses, amiable company . . . without quarrels, war, or poverty.

It sounds good, doesn't it? But then he says, **I am not mocking this mentality, not at all, but have we considered the significance of death?** He's making the important point that holding on to our ideals doesn't leave any room for the chaos that is inevitable in life. There's no place for failure, for death and impermanence.

He compares our predicament of wanting to find lasting satisfaction to watching the beauty of a sunrise: **We watch the sun become redder and redder, finally turning into white light, bright sunshine. One would prefer to hold on to the dawn and sunrise, to keep the sun from rising completely, to hold on to the glowing promise. We would prefer to do this, but we cannot.**

As Thinley Norbu Rinpoche said, "There is no perfect in this samsara." The truth of impermanence ensures that there's never really a final summing up, only continual change. This is something I think we can all rely on and accept as true, even though we live our life as if we could get it to pause on "friendly."

From here, Rinpoche presents a traditional teaching on the three kinds of suffering: all-pervading pain, the pain of alternation, and the pain of pain. *Cutting Through Spiritual Materialism* describes the experience of all-pervading suffering as "the constantly repeated feeling that something is lacking, incomplete in our lives." It's a feeling that things are never quite right. Rather than relax with our life as we experience it, we struggle.

In his book *The Truth of Suffering and the Path of Liberation*, Rinpoche describes all-pervading pain as "the subtle sense of general misery and dissatisfaction that goes on all the time." He says that this suffering "is connected with constant movement: flickering thoughts, latching onto one situation after another, or constantly changing subjects. It is like getting out of a car and walking into a building, and getting out of the building and walking into a car, and being hungry and settling down in a restaurant and eating food, and going back. . . . We are never fully satisfied."

But instead of struggling against what's showing up at our door, instead of being "me against" or "me for" our experience, we could join in and work with our everyday circumstances, no matter how difficult they may be. "Struggle," Rinpoche says in *Cutting Through Spiritual Materialism*, "is the root of suffering."

We can develop an appetite for life as it is rather than for life as we want it to be. This is a big shift, but until we make it, suffering will continue for a simple reason—we want things to be different from how they are. We prefer permanent stability, security, and reliability, but this is impossible. The very first talk by Rinpoche that I ever went to was in San Francisco. He sat down and didn't say a word for what seemed like an eternity, letting his gaze move slowly around the room. Then his first words were, "It's best if you can realize right from the start that you'll never be able to get it all together."

All-pervading pain, Rinpoche says, **is inevitable as long as there is the presence of discontinuity and insecurity**. We want stability and security, not only now and again but as a final resting place. We hold on to this unrealistic hope and, as a result, we suffer.

The second type of suffering is the pain of alternation. This overlaps with all-pervading suffering but zeroes in on the continual alternation we experience between "I like" and "I don't like," between things working out and not working out. Sometimes our experience is pleasant, and sometimes it hurts. It keeps alternating, never coming to a final rest on either side.

Over the years, my close students have written to tell me about their practice and their lives. A typical scenario goes like this: At first there's nothing but pain. They're distraught because they're going through a messy divorce. I feel for them, but I know how impermanent our life situations are. A year and half later, they've found a new partner and they're on top of the world. Now life is as it should be. Everything—relationship, children, job, health—is going smoothly. I'm happy for them, but I also know that no circumstances are final. Then their health deteriorates and one of the children starts acting out. Up and down it goes until at some point, because of their practice, the student begins to have more equilibrium. Pain and pleasure continue to alternate, but the student doesn't go up and down with the outer circumstances in the way they used to. They move closer to "being okay with not being okay," as Tsoknyi Rinpoche puts it.

In "Styles of Imprisonment," the next chapter of *The Myth of Freedom*, Rinpoche describes the six realms of samsara. In the hell realm, one's experience *does* seem to pause permanently on unrelenting suffering. Like everything else, this experience is impermanent, but it feels like it lasts for all eternity and there's no way out.

The opposite situation is the god realm. This is what we've all been seeking, a promised land where we have everything: wealth, beauty, strength, intelligence, comfortable outer circumstances, a contented state of mind. Life is smooth and good, and there's no suffering at all. It seems to go on forever.

Yet the god-realm experience is also impermanent. When one has everything together and never questions that this is how it will always be, the pain of losing that is extremely intense. It's like when a movie star or athlete who has been on top of the world, adored by all, suffers a dramatic fall from grace.

For those of us in the human realm, there's some good news about the pain of alternation, about knowing the taste of both pleasure and pain. We have just enough comfort to allow us to realize our predicament and seek a way out. And we have enough pain to inspire us to get out as fast as we can.

The pain of alternation might seem obvious, but somehow we tend to miss it. You could experiment for the rest of your life and see if anything ever stops alternating. Actually, your next meditation session would be an excellent time to test this.

The third kind of suffering is called "the pain of pain," which Rinpoche describes as **the pain of all those life situations you do not want**. The Buddha was referring to this when he taught on the suffering of birth, old age, sickness, and death, as well as "the pain of not getting what we want," "the pain of not being able to hold on to what we have," and "the pain of getting what we don't want." We are certainly familiar with all of these.

The pain of pain is, I imagine, what most of us think of as "suffering": bad things happening to ourselves and others, one on top of another. Rinpoche describes a situation where suffering escalates: **You are already insecure, feeling uncertain about your territory. On top of that, you worry about your condition and develop an ulcer. While rushing to the doctor to treat the ulcer, you stub your toe. Resisting pain only increases its intensity.**

That's the main message—avoidance makes matters worse. There's just one misfortune after another, and the more we struggle, the worse it gets. In this section, Rinpoche's example of taking a trip to Paris, where everything possible goes wrong, always makes me laugh. It describes the pain of pain well—though compared to the pain of those living in poverty, of those whose lives are torn apart by war, famine, prejudice, and natural disasters, it seems like an extremely lightweight example.

The three kinds of suffering are characteristic of all living beings, but particularly of us human beings. They are part of what it means to be born human. Not only do we deny the shifting, changing condition of life but we also have a deep-seated habitual tendency to try to get ground under our feet. Even as we become more comfortable with impermanence, we still do our darndest to grasp onto something.

Having nothing to hold on to is exceedingly nerve-racking. According to the Buddhist teachings, our tendency to grasp stays with us even through the stages of the bodhisattva path, which Rinpoche discusses in chapter 6. It's so involuntary that it has to wear itself out, which doesn't fully happen until we attain Buddhahood. Knowing this, maybe you can give yourself a break for just being human.

EGOLESSNESS

ALMOST ALL people on the planet experience themselves as permanent, ongoing beings. In this section, Rinpoche gives one of the most fundamental Buddhist teachings, a teaching that refutes this assumption. **The sense of continuity and solidity of self,** he says, **is an illusion.**

We feel as if we're solid and permanent, but that is a misperception. There is only a succession of rapidly passing moments that we can't hold on to. Rinpoche says, therefore, that **we cannot hold on to me and mine and make them solid things**. The view of "me and mine" is based on a misunderstanding. We misperceive ourselves as solid, but our body is mostly water. We misperceive that we're permanent, that the self we were yesterday is the same self we are today, but our body—every atom of our body—is constantly changing.

Our thoughts also have never stopped flowing. This discovery has shocked new meditators for millennia. No matter how we try to calm it down, the mind is often like a wild horse, a restless monkey, a rampaging elephant. The thoughts just keep coming and changing and moving. So instead of having our usual sense of self, it's more accurate to experience ourselves as in process. We are, forever, in process. We do perceive and think and feel. We *are* individuals. But we are not fixed, static individuals.

In fact, nothing in this world ever stays fixed. Even the door of your room has changed since yesterday. You don't have to come home and find it painted red to know that. It's like a pencil: It appears not to change, and then suddenly it's a stub. Impermanence is one thing we can count on.

Rinpoche compares the illusory self to a movie in which **the individual film frames are played so quickly that they generate the illusion of continual movement**. In the same way, he says, **we build up an idea, a preconception, that self and other are solid and continuous.**

The nonexistence of a solid, ongoing self is known as "egolessness." To return to the grain-of-sand analogy, if we don't overcrowd or obstruct anything with a big sense of "me," we enjoy a sense of spaciousness. There's a feeling of tremendous room, a feeling of infinite possibilities. The less ego one has, the more one can relax and appreciate the world and other beings. It's like what the singer-songwriter Leonard Cohen said after many years of Zen meditation. After all that practice, he got bored to death with all his ego dramas and they started to fall away. Then he found that "the less there was of me, the happier I got."

There are two stages, Rinpoche says, **to understanding egolessness. In the first stage, we perceive that ego does not exist as a solid entity.** This is the stage I have been discussing. The second stage goes deeper. Here we recognize the illusory nature of all our solidly held concepts, all our cherished views and opinions, all our erroneous conceptions about self and phenomena.

As a species, we make a big deal about our view of things. Even if we understand to some degree that there is no solid, permanent self, **we still have formulated a subtle concept of egolessness**. We have made our conceptual understanding of egolessness into a credential. Rinpoche says that we can use our understanding of words and ideas to obscure a genuine experience of egolessness. We take Buddhist concepts such as emptiness, or even teachings on suffering—anything we think we understand—and use them to feel secure and safe. **This is just cheap escapism,** he says. It's just another way of avoiding the unpindownable quality of our experience.

When we try to impose philosophical concepts onto our experience of life, they don't always fit. When we're actually suffering, Rinpoche asks us, can we get away from that with our philosophical views? **There is no one to suffer, so who cares? If you suffer it must be your illusion.** But as he points out, **when we actually suffer, can we remain indifferent? Of course not; suffering is stronger than our petty opinions.** I remember clearly reading that for the first time, and the impression it made on me. His words struck me as being such a simple, clear, down-to-earth way of cutting through intellectualizing and honoring direct experience.

He goes on to say that **a true understanding of egolessness cuts through opinion. The absence of a notion of egolessness**—in other words, the absence of a solid *belief* in egolessness—**allows us to fully experience pain, birth, and death because then there are no philosophical paddings.**

We can use Buddhist teachings to build up our ego and distance ourselves from reality rather than put us more in touch. Instead of moving closer to the ungraspable nature of experience, we can go with the strong, futile human tendency to try to pin everything down. But Rinpoche makes the point that we can only fully experience the ups and downs of life when we drop all of our fixed ideas—about ego, egolessness, and everything else.

Suzuki Roshi admired what he called "beginner's mind." "In the beginner's mind," he said, "there are many possibilities. In the expert's mind, there are few." Rinpoche enjoyed working with his American students because, for the most part, though there were certainly scholars among us, we were the opposite of experts. We had zero preconceptions about Buddhism.

I, for instance, knew absolutely nothing about what I was getting into. Rinpoche's words addressed the suffering I was experiencing, and that was it. Honestly, he could have been Hindu, Sufi, or no religion at all, for all I cared. I was just drawn to the truth of what he was saying. We students may have been confused, trippy, and untamed, but when it came to Buddhism, we had the beginner's mind—that fresh mind, free of fixed ideas—and Rinpoche liked it.

This second stage of egolessness is important to understand because we don't only have solid ideas about Buddhist teachings. We have solid ideas about everything. It helps us when we begin to see that our views and opinions, our personal take on things, are just that—only our ideas and opinions, not the absolute truth.

Rinpoche would use the expression "free from fixed mind." That is an apt description of the second stage of egolessness. **The whole idea is that we must drop all reference points, all concepts of what is or what should be,** he said.

Whatever happens, pleasure and pain, birth and death . . . are experienced in their fullest flavor. Whether they are sweet or sour, they are experienced completely, without philosophical overlays or emotional attitudes to make things seem lovable or presentable.

Q&A

Throughout the book I include questions from the audience that were asked during the original teachings I gave on *The Myth of Freedom* in 2007.

Q: Living in Berkeley, I see lots of examples of spiritual materialism. People say, "I found the greatest teaching," and "This is the best." I struggle with this, and I see that as a Westerner, there's this desire to find the most select club and the best team and to know you're the winner. But I also see some Asian teachers who act similarly. It doesn't seem like just a Western phenomenon.

PEMA: Spiritual materialism is definitely not just a Western phenomenon. But the main thing is to look for it in yourself. Try to see where you might do that. In this case, a person might feel subtly smug about not doing what these people you describe are doing. You could build up your ego with the pride of not being like one of them. Do you see what I mean? It's a slippery slope.

From when we first connect with Buddhism, through years of meditation and digging deeply into the teachings, it takes a while to really be able to have the kind of compassionate self-reflection where you can smell your own rat without freaking out. It's a gradual process of developing loving-kindness toward yourself, rather than self-denigration.

All these ways in which we close our minds toward other people, for this reason or that reason, are just prejudice, a kind of fundamentalism. This is exactly what Rinpoche is talking about—holding on to opinions as a way to secure yourself. It's very subtle and we all do it.

TWO

STYLES OF IMPRISONMENT

COSMIC JOKE

THE SECOND CHAPTER of *The Myth of Freedom* has seven sections and deals primarily with the six realms of samsara. Rinpoche referred to these as the six **styles of imprisonment**. The first section, "Cosmic Joke," serves as an entrance into this topic. Here Rinpoche describes how ego develops in terms of **the five *skandhas*, a set of Buddhist concepts which describe ego as a five-step process**. I think of this section as a close look at how we got into this mess.

How did ego come to be, and how did it escalate into our ongoing experience of samsara? Samsara refers to the suffering that results from repeating the same habitual patterns over and over and over again. From moment to moment, from year to year, for whole lifetimes, we come up with ways to avoid pain and to seek and hold on to pleasure. In so doing, we poor, predictable beings keep our discontent alive and well.

Rinpoche said that the first step on the spiritual path is to realize we're stuck. He emphasized seeing our confusion clearly before fantasizing about love and light. So "Cosmic Joke" begins, **In order to cut through the ambition of ego, we must understand how we set up me and my territory, how we use our projections as credentials to prove our existence. The source of the effort to confirm our solidity is an uncertainty as to whether or not we exist.**

He spends the rest of the section describing our ongoing effort to **prove our own existence by finding a reference point outside ourselves, something with which to have a relationship, something solid to feel separate from**. The resultant **sense of the solidity of I and other** is a **gigantic hoax**, which all of us tend to fall for. This hoax is the fundamental dualistic fixation that governs our lives, what he later refers to as **the dualistic barrier**.

Rinpoche describes our futile, all-too-human attempts to confirm our separateness and solidity and to find something predictable and secure to hold on to. Instead of growing our capacity to relax with the groundlessness of our predicament, we do what's predictable and hold on for dear life.

What he portrays here is our extreme discomfort with things not being sum-up-able. As he puts it, **We do not realize that the whole process** of trying to avoid groundlessness **is unnecessary, that we do not need a floor to stand on. . . . There was never any danger of falling.** In fact, trying to secure our ground is **the biggest joke of all, a cosmic joke**.

Ultimately there is nothing to hold on to. My experience as a practitioner, however, is that in the beginning, we do need things to hold on to. But we also understand that we're moving toward letting go and away from holding on. At the same time, we have to know our current limitations. And for now, most of us need something like the teachings and the meditation technique to hold on to. These things are like a raft that will take us across the river, but once we're on the other side, we'll leave the raft behind.

When we rely on the meditation technique, for instance, we follow the instructions about how to relate to breath and thoughts. We are faithful to the technique. However, these instructions are intended to guide us toward more ease and flexibility, not make us more rigid and dogmatic about the right way to meditate.

Whatever practice you do, you just start where you are, and you work with that. But the process is one of opening to your emotional states, opening beyond fixed views and opinions, opening to life as it is. You're moving toward shedding your outdated propensities without collecting anything new. If this is your intention, then there's no problem with temporarily holding on as a way to move forward.

Rinpoche explains how we perpetuate the hoax of solidity and duality through the five-step process called the five skandhas. "In terms of the notion of self, we are not actually one individual entity per se," Rinpoche writes in *The Truth of Suffering and the Path of Liberation*, "but just a collection of what are known as the five skandhas, or five heaps of being."

The Buddha broke down our sense of being an individual entity into five skandhas: form, feeling, perception, concept, and consciousness. The way this is usually taught is that you try to find a self in each of these five categories. You begin with the skandha of form, with your body. Can I find a self in my hand? Can I find a self in my head? Or in my heart? Then you move on to the rest of the skandhas. Can I find a self in my feelings? Or in my perceptions? Or in my conceptual ideas about how things are? Finally, you try to find a self in your consciousness. This way of teaching the skandhas is a vehicle for dismantling the illusion of self. You break it down until you can really see that the self is nothing continuous and solid. It's continually arising and perishing, arising again and perishing again.

But in this chapter, Rinpoche teaches the skandhas differently. He teaches them in a style that belongs to the Dzogchen tradition. **In the beginning,** he says, **there is open space.** From that open, fluid space, we experience things getting more and more solid. Usually this happens in an uncatchable instant, but you can slow the process down and look at it very closely. The first thing that happens is we perceive "other." Instead of remaining one with the fluidity of space, we instinctively separate ourselves from that openness and solidify it as out there, as something different. This is how Rinpoche describes the skandha of form.

Rinpoche sometimes refers to this first skandha not just as "form" but as **ignorance/form**. The basic ignorance is that we set ourselves apart from everything else. This illusion of separateness is the beginning of dualism and the birth of ego, where the cycle of our dissatisfaction begins.

The five skandhas happen in a rapid chain reaction. In the beginning, it's hard to distinguish where one ends and the next begins. For instance, as soon as we experience the skandha of form and the initial feeling of separateness, we experience without fail the second skandha, **feeling**. They seem inseparable. In his book *Wake Up to Your Life*, my friend Ken McLeod gives the example of hearing your coworker's voice and instantly having a subtle, nonverbal reaction. Even ordinary people like ourselves, who aren't necessarily great meditators, can notice these subtle reactions. You're sitting at a table and someone you don't like sits down next to you, and you feel yourself subtly withdraw and contract. But if you like the person, you feel a subtle opening or even grasping, a nonverbal "I'm glad you sat here." Or you could simply react with indifference.

This simple practice of noticing your reactions is a game changer. I do a practice where I note "comfortable," "uncomfortable," or "neutral," and try to leave it there. I acknowledge being "for" or "against" or "neutral," but without the spin-off. Feeling doesn't have to set off a chain reaction, but unfortunately for us, it usually does.

Then, right away, comes the third skandha, which Rinpoche calls **impulse/perception** and Ken calls "interpretation." This third skandha is still somewhat preverbal, but we've gone from the subtle gut feeling of the second skandha—your stomach tightening or loosening, contracting or expanding—to the interpretation of "like" or "don't like." Ken says that at this third skandha level, you can also have subtle perceptions such as being flattered or insulted. But, very importantly, there's no storyline yet. You haven't inflamed it yet, so this is a place at the pre-thought level where you can interrupt the whole thing—but of course, only if you're aware it's happening.

It is our thoughts that fuel our suffering. This description of the development of ego tells us how the process starts with just a little blip—a little pulling away, moving toward, or being indifferent—and next thing you know, there's a full-blown drama, the source of all wars, all domestic violence, all suffering in the world. As Rinpoche taught, "It quickly goes from minute to expansive."

After the third skandha level of "like" and "don't like," we get to the fourth skandha, **concept**. Here we start to build a case, and thoughts start coming in. It's still subtle. But along with "like" or "don't like," there is now labeling. Basically, we get more into it. It's a little more loaded. Now we use terms like *ugly* or *beautiful*, *right* or *wrong*, *acceptable* or *unacceptable*. **We begin to categorize things,** Rinpoche says, **putting them into certain pigeonholes.** It's easier to see this here than in the third skandha because it's so blatant. But because the momentum is escalating, it's also harder to interrupt. It's harder, but definitely possible.

From here the process moves quickly into **consciousness**, the fifth skandha. This is where we generally find ourselves, with full-blown thoughts and emotions, strongly held views and opinions. Rinpoche says, **We need a very active and efficient mechanism to keep the instinctive and intellectual processes of ego coordinated.** This, he says, is the job of consciousness.

The reactivity is up and running, going strong. But the important thing to remember is that there's always space available. The beauty of this teaching is that you can interrupt the momentum at any point and reconnect with natural openness.

Because we have such a deep-seated habit of grabbing on and holding tight, we miss the natural openness that's always present. Rinpoche gives meditation as the way to see the transparency of the whole progression of the skandhas. We start at the end of the process, at the most outer, gross, accessible level. We start with seeing our thoughts and emotions, and how charged they are with "this" and "that," "like" and "don't like"—and so forth.

Then if we trace back the development of ego through the skandhas, we find that the further back we go, the subtler and less graspable the experience becomes. The very good news is that at any moment of our lives, we can experience the open state that existed before the dualistic progression began, before we became afraid and started seeking something solid to grasp onto.

To review: With the skandha of form, Rinpoche says that **when a gap or space occurs in our experience of mind, then there is a sudden glimpse of awareness, openness, ab-**

sence of self. But we are unnerved by this and pull back into trying to find solidity. He describes this so simply as, **We want to hold on to something.** This is **the source of karmic chain reactions.** The chain reaction begins as soon as we pull back and start to have a sense of solid me and solid other. Here we are not talking about "once upon a time" but what we do continually.

With the skandha of feeling, our experience becomes further solidified with a sense of "for" or "against." With the third skandha of perception, there's further interpretation of like and dislike, of passion (grasping) and aggression (pushing away). The third potential reaction at this stage is indifference, where **we numb any sensitive areas that we want to avoid, that we think might hurt us.**

With the fourth skandha of concept, it's not so subtle anymore. We build a case with ideas such as "ugly/bad, beautiful/good." With the fifth skandha, consciousness, our thoughts and emotions are going strong, and we get swept away. As Rinpoche says, **Consciousness consists of emotions and irregular thought patterns, all of which taken together form the different fantasy worlds with which we occupy ourselves. These fantasy worlds are referred to in the scriptures as the "six realms."** This is the subject of the rest of this chapter.

However, before commenting on the six sections that follow, I'd like to discuss the topic of realms altogether. In the traditional Buddhist teachings, there are six realms: the hell realm, the hungry ghost realm, the animal realm, the human realm, the jealous god (or *asura*) realm, and the god realm. But what exactly is a realm? Is it an actual place or is it a psychological state?

In the next section, Rinpoche explains it this way: **We dwell within a particular version of reality. We are fascinated with maintaining familiar surroundings, familiar desires and longings, so as not to give in to a spacious state of mind.**

In his book *Penetrating Wisdom*, Dzogchen Ponlop Rinpoche says that a realm is a "group experience of shared karma"—an experience shared in common with every being of that realm. In the human realm, for example, although there are many differences, we all experience it in a similar way. If I say, "Look at that mountain," we can all look and see it. We experience a common world with sky above and earth below. On the other hand, the common experiences of beings in the other realms are totally unlike ours. We can't even conceive of what a fish or worm experiences.

In his book *Fearless Simplicity*, Tsoknyi Rinpoche says that "we are all born into some sort of group dream; we are group dreaming." This is true of all the different realms: hell beings dream the hell realm, jealous gods dream the jealous god realm, humans dream the human realm, and so forth. In *The Tibetan Book of Living and Dying*, Sogyal Rinpoche writes that how we perceive the world depends entirely on our karmic vision: "What we see is what our karmic vision allows us to see, and no more."

A classic teaching on how beings of different realms perceive reality uses water as an example. Humans see water as something for drinking or bathing; for fish, water is a home, a total environment; for gods, it's nectar; for jealous gods, a weapon; for hungry ghosts, pus and blood; for hell beings, molten lava.

My insight into realms comes from having been with a friend when she was having a psychotic break. I stood right in front of her, and her eyes were wide open, but for her I was not there. She was conversing with someone I could not see, describing a whole world I could not see. We were in the same room but in totally different realms. After that, I stopped believing that there was one true, inherent reality.

If I were in a room with a dog, an insect, and a bird, none of us would have the same experience of reality. We would all be in different realms. As Ken says, we would be in different "worlds projected by our reactive emotions."

Sogyal Rinpoche asks a question that I find provocative: "How can we possibly say definitively what does or does not exist beyond the bounds of our limited vision?" Trungpa Rinpoche calls the realms "group hallucinations," but he adds that it's not helpful to say they don't exist because for those that live there, they are completely real. This is what he means by **styles of imprisonment**: We are imprisoned by our limited vision.

The way I see it, the teachers who speak of the realms as if they are real and those who describe them as psychological states are not in opposition; they are simply speaking from different points of view. As Sogyal Rinpoche says, "We can see that the six realms definitely do exist. They exist in the way we unconsciously allow our negative emotions to project and crystallize entire realms around us."

Some teachers emphasize the interdependence between our psychological states and the places in which we find ourselves. Rinpoche did this at times as well, and I find this view to be appealing. But all the teachers present the realms—and suffering as a whole—as places or states you can escape from. There would be no point to teach suffering in such depth if it wasn't followed by teachings on the cessation of suffering.

In *The Myth of Freedom*, Rinpoche taught the realms in a unique way that has had quite an influence on others. **The realms are predominantly emotional attitudes toward ourselves and our surroundings,** he said. He spoke of them as places not where we are reborn but where we find ourselves right now. **As human beings we may, during the course of a day, experience the emotions of all the realms, from the pride of the god realm to the hatred and paranoia of the hell realm.**

Each of the realms has a key emotion, and when that emotion is functioning strongly, we are essentially in that realm. However, we all have one realm in which we dwell more consistently. As Rinpoche put it, **A person's psychology is usually firmly rooted in one realm. This realm provides us with a style of confusion, a way of entertaining and occupying ourselves so as not to have to face our fundamental uncertainty, our ultimate fear that we may not exist.**

Let me give an overview of the six realms here and then go into more detail afterward. When rage and hatred are functioning strongly, you are essentially in the hell realm. More traditional teachings would say that if you die with a mind full of rage and hatred, you'll be born in the physical environment of hell. It's not like punishment; it's just where rage and hatred take us.

The key emotion of the hungry ghost realm is usually called "greed" or "avarice." It's a hunger that can never be satisfied. When that hunger is functioning strongly, you're essentially in the hungry ghost realm. In the traditional iconography, the poor creatures have tiny mouths, extremely long and narrow throats, and huge bellies. It's hard to get enough food or drink down to fill up the belly. I think many of us can understand what this image is pointing to and what that feels like.

In the animal realm, the emotion is a kind of dullness that results in compulsive behavior. You need to keep things the same, keep them predictable. Rinpoche talks about this as a psychological state, but the traditional presentation refers to literal animals. In this realm, you're only comfortable if things fit within what you know. When things are unpredictable, you become confused and afraid.

In the human realm, the emotion of passion is central. You experience this as wanting, craving, needing, grasping. When these emotions are active, you are effectively in the human realm.

When the emotion of competitiveness or envy is functioning, that's the experience of the jealous god realm. For the god realm, Rinpoche stresses self-absorption. I don't know what the emotion is exactly, but it's a quality of resting complacently in comfort, with an attitude of superiority. Traditionally it's referred to as pride.

Now I will go through these realms in more detail while still trying to keep it simple. In talking about each realm, I will point out the "style of imprisonment" that we use to seek ground and security. Then I'll give basic statements about each of the realms, which come from Ken McLeod.

SELF-ABSORPTION

TRADITIONALLY THE six realms are depicted in a circle cut into six pie slices: three on the top (gods, jealous gods, humans), three on the bottom (animals, hungry ghosts, hell beings). The top and the bottom are referred to as the higher and lower realms, respectively.

In "Self-Absorption," Rinpoche begins at the top, with the god realm. The life of the gods is the realm that we seek—innocently and naively. It's a seamless life of happiness, pleasure, and comfort, with no pain. How amazing it is to have a teaching on this as a style of suffering!

To get a feeling for the god realm, think *Downton Abbey* before the Second World War, or in more recent times, Elon Musk—a person who has everything money can buy, including power and influence, and seemingly never doubts that he's on top and that what he thinks and does is the obvious, absolute way things should be.

In this realm, you already have it made. You have the sense of privilege, beauty, and entitlement being your birthright. You live in the world of good taste and elegance. For you, this is just how life is. But from the outside, it's the world of the "beautiful people." Ken McLeod says that the basic statement about the god realm is "I'm right, and that's just how it is."

You might say, "I don't hear anything bad about this yet." However, one of the downsides of the realm is that it's impossible to stand in the shoes of people who are suffering deeply. It's impossible to feel what it would be like to experience war, to have no shelter, to be in prison, to spend the entire day searching for food, or all the multitude of ways in which people suffer. Suffering can have the advantage of helping us to have empathy.

Eventually the seamless pleasure of the god realm ends because impermanence and death are characteristic of all six realms, of all life as we know it. When the god-realm experience comes to an end, the suffering is more intense than in the hell realms. The bubble was so complete—there was no doubt, no hint that it would ever end. You just took it for granted that it would last forever. As Rinpoche writes, **The realm of the gods is not particularly painful, in itself. The pain comes from the eventual disillusionment. You think you have achieved a continually blissful state, spiritual or worldly; you are dwelling on that. But suddenly something shakes you and you realize that what you have achieved is not going to last forever.**

I once met a young woman who had grown up in Iran, in a family that was close with the Shah. She was around eight years old when the Shah was overthrown and in her twenties when we met. She had spent her childhood in an enchanted world. She lived in a magnificent palace, and her family's estate had acres and acres of beautiful parkland. This life was all she ever knew. Then suddenly, while her parents were in Paris, the revolution began. By a miracle, she and her siblings got out, but her magical life was gone forever. Overnight it turned upside down.

As Rinpoche presents it, you might be in that psychological state right now. You don't believe your privileged, comfortable life will ever end. I've known a few young people who have made millions in the tech industry but seem completely out of touch. Everything is the best, and they don't even think about not going to certain clubs and resorts, not having a beautiful house or houses, never having to look at the price tag, waking up and going to bed in comfort and luxury.

They never consider that their lifestyle, health, and great circumstances are not permanent. But all this could be undone if they learned that their partner or child had incurable cancer. Suddenly it would be—*boom!*—all over. It doesn't take a stock market crash. Just life itself will do it.

Rinpoche talks about the god realm in two ways. One is based on material comfort and lifestyle, as I just described. The other, which he emphasizes more in *The Myth of Freedom*, is using the spiritual practice to get high, to have altered states, to stay in some kind of bliss state. That was pretty rampant in the sixties and seventies and probably still is. It's the idea of eternal ecstasy built on spiritual practice. Both of these versions of the god realm, Rinpoche says, are impermanent and destined to end. There may be no pain for many years, but ultimately you can't keep it going. You might even feel you've attained enlightenment. But when that high dissipates, despair and depression can set in.

PARANOIA

THE NEXT REALM, that of the jealous gods, Rinpoche calls "paranoia." Sometimes the key emotion is described as "envy," but paranoia really gets at it. If this emotion is functioning, you're essentially in the jealous god realm. For some people—maybe you or someone close to you—this emotion runs your life.

When you have the jealous god mentality, you have wealth, success, and so forth, and other people think you have it made, but you're paranoid that someone else has it better. Your way of scrambling for ground and security—rather than staying with the fluid, unpredictable quality of open space—is trying to win, to engage in one-upmanship.

The dominant characteristic of the jealous god or asura realm is paranoia, Rinpoche says. **If you are trying to help someone who has an asura mentality, they interpret your action as an attempt to oppress them or infiltrate their territory. But if you decide not to help them, they interpret that as a selfish act: you are seeking comfort for yourself. If you present both alternatives to them, then they think you are playing games with them. The asura mentality is quite intelligent: it sees all the hidden corners.**

With an asura mentality, you are always looking to see how you're doing in relationship to somebody else. Ken McLeod says this realm is like a warring nation, where you always feel that the other side has more power, so you fight harder and harder. The suffering here comes from competitiveness.

The basic statement is “I’m better than you,” but you don’t really believe it. It’s not like the god realm, where you have no doubt about your position. In the jealous god realm, you’re always trying to prove that you’re better, and you’re paranoid that you aren’t.

PASSION

THEN THERE'S the human realm, the realm that you and I inhabit physically. But since Rinpoche taught that we spend time in all the realms, we can also think of the human realm as a psychological state.

The basic statement of the human realm is "If I can just get *that,* then I'll be fine. If I can get a loving relationship, enough money, and my dream job, I'll finally feel satisfied." Your life revolves around being with people you like, avoiding people you don't like, getting what you want, keeping what you have, and avoiding getting what you don't want. Does all that sound familiar?

How you seek ground and security is generally geared toward the future. If you could just make the right move, the right choices, *then* you could relax. But you may have noticed that this relaxation only lasts a short time, if it happens at all.

Traditionally it is said that the human realm is the ideal place to get out of the **styles of imprisonment** altogether—to be free of cycling through the repetitive pattern of trying to escape where you are. When there's too much pleasure, as in the god realm, it never occurs to you to escape. You aren't struggling; you're just cruising.

In the lower realms, which we'll come to next, the suffering is so intense that you have no room to look into the causes of suffering and find freedom from the whole cycle.

In the human realm, there can be just enough suffering to spur you on to find an answer. That's certainly what drove me to look for a spiritual path. I was looking for a way to deal with the suffering I was experiencing when my husband left me. At the same time, I had enough comfort in my human life to take a bigger view of my predicament and look for answers.

Having this mixture of pain and pleasure, as well as the ability to empathize with others, is why Rinpoche says in *Cutting Through Spiritual Materialism*, "It is in the human realm that the possibility of breaking the karmic chain, or the circle of samsara, arises. The intellect of the human realm and the possibility of discriminating action allow room to question the whole process of struggle."

STUPIDITY

WITH THE ANIMAL realm, we enter the so-called lower realms. They are called "lower" to indicate that the suffering is far more intense than in the higher realms of gods, jealous gods, and humans.

Rinpoche uses the term *stupidity*, which animal lovers, such as myself, don't like. But it doesn't really mean that animals are stupid. We know at the level of instinct that they are actually very smart. I've often been outsmarted by squirrels, not to mention all other kinds of rodents. Once I even tried to outsmart ants. I thought, "I'll find out what they like and then make a trail that takes them away from the kitchen." I tried sugar, but these ants didn't like sugar. I tried all kinds of things but couldn't find one that worked. But the minute I turned around, they covered the counters. And with squirrels, if you've ever tried to keep them out of a bird feeder, then you know at that level they are definitely a lot smarter than you are.

When Rinpoche says "stupidity," he's referring to the way that an animal—and we ourselves when we're in this psychological state—seeks ground and security through predictability and routine. The idea is to follow the rules, to keep the status quo. **The animal quality of mind,** Rinpoche says, **is a mentality which stubbornly pushes forward toward predetermined**

goals. When animals are in a situation where they can do things automatically and instinctually, they're extremely skillful and competent. But it throws them for a loop when their familiar systems break down. It's so sad to see an animal out of its element, not knowing what to do.

The suffering of animals is a subject that's very dear to my heart. We pamper dogs in the United States, but all you have to do is go to an impoverished country to see how terribly dogs and cats suffer. Compared to them, our pets are in a god realm. But even your god-realm dog waits around all day for you to take it for a walk. It lives for the moment that it can go outside or when a scrap might fall off the table.

There is a traditional meditation where you try to put yourself in the shoes of the beings in other realms. You can imagine what it's like to be your dog or cat; the fragile little insects; the fish and the birds; the rodents who are terrified of being eaten and scamper around all day long, collecting, collecting, collecting. You can do this with beings in all the realms.

For the animal state of mind, Ken McLeod's basic statement is "I'm just trying to survive." If you experience that mentality, the key thing is to be where you are, completely and fully, without struggling against it but also without acting out. Just get the taste and smell of where you are.

Have you ever been in a dream where you're trying to get away, and you struggle, struggle, struggle? My childhood friend Suzy had a recurring nightmare about monsters chasing her. She'd open a door and slam it behind her, and then she'd hear the monsters open it. She kept going through endless corridors with doors opening and shutting, and the monsters always coming after her. One day I asked her, "What do they look like?" She said, "I don't know, I'm always running." That must have planted some kind of seed in her mind because the next time it happened, she turned around. It took a lot of courage, but she got curious about what they looked like, and as soon as she turned, they started to dissolve.

This was one of Rinpoche's recurrent messages: If you want to find the gaps in your suffering and have glimpses of open space, then don't struggle to get away from where you are. Connect with the immediacy of your experience.

POVERTY

IN THE HUNGRY ghost realm, you experience poverty. It's not necessarily that you lack money or shelter, but you have the mentality of neediness—what Rinpoche calls "poverty mentality." As he writes, **It is painful to be suspended in unfulfilled desire, continually searching for satisfaction.**

The basic statement for this realm is "I'm taking everything." You feel the need to take as much as possible because you never feel you have enough. Perhaps you seek ground and security through hoarding and stealing, but that doesn't bring you contentment. As Rinpoche says, even if you get what you want, **after a while you become restless again and look for something else to consume.**

The traditional presentation says something I've always found helpful. When the emotion of poverty mentality is working, you perceive your environment as barren. The world you inhabit can never give you enough food, water, clothing, or gratification of any kind. Your poverty seems to come from your environment, but these teachings say that "not enough" is actually a state of mind. Rinpoche says, **Fundamentally, you feel poor.**

When you're born into a situation where you really have nothing, poverty mentality could understandably be part of that birth. But there are many people who have hardly anything—in terms of money, food, and so forth—and are not in this realm. They have some kind of inner strength and resilience where they don't feel fundamentally poor. To free yourself of poverty mentality means connecting with a fundamental richness that isn't based on outer things. Otherwise, as Rinpoche says, **there is always some sense of inadequacy**.

At the outer level, the world never seems to give you enough. But at the inner level, you can't even enjoy what you have. You can be in the middle of great plenty, but for one reason or another, you can't enjoy it and you still feel needy. As the Rolling Stones sang, "I can't get no satisfaction." The jealous gods also have this poverty mentality, but it's nowhere near as intense as it is for the hungry ghosts.

I had a little taste of this when I had a stomach condition. Whenever I would eat, I would have pain, indigestion, and heartburn. At the same time, I was always hungry. I was told not to eat after 4:30 p.m., which I adhered to faithfully, but I was ravenous. Then I thought about the hungry ghost realm and felt some empathy. It gave me a little taste of how painful it would be to continually dwell in this realm. His Holiness the Dalai Lama has suggested periodically skipping dinner or not eating for a whole day to have a sense of what it's like to be someone with no food at all.

In the human realm, when the suffering gets bad enough, people often start to ask questions. But in the hungry ghost realm, the poverty and greed are so intense that you don't ask any questions. You just try to steal more, hoard more, struggle more as a way to escape your neediness. You stay stuck in a vicious cycle, a cycle of pain.

Your very methods of trying to get ground and security are what keep you stuck in that bubble reality, that fantasy world that you call your life. That's why Rinpoche called the realms **styles of imprisonment**. But it's self-imprisonment. No one else is imprisoning you.

Ken McLeod offers a clear explanation of how to leave this hungry ghost style of imprisonment behind: "When you can stay present in the experience of neediness, you die to the hungry ghost realm." You develop, he says, "an increased capacity to let the feelings of needing this or that come and go. The actual feeling of neediness carries less charge, and you don't feel the compulsion to act on it."

ANGER

THE TRADITIONAL texts describe the hell realms vividly. In Patrul Rinpoche's *The Words of My Perfect Teacher*, for instance, he describes eighteen hells, one more horrendous than the next. In *Cutting Through Spiritual Materialism*, Rinpoche describes walking through gigantic fields of red-hot iron, or being marked with black lines and cut apart. "These and other hallucinations of hell," he writes, "are generated from an environment of claustrophobia and aggression."

In *The Myth of Freedom*, Rinpoche writes that in the hell realm, **you cannot really eliminate pain through aggression. The more you kill, the more you strengthen the killer, who will create new things to be killed. The aggression grows until finally there is no space: the whole environment has been solidified. There are not even gaps in which to look back or do a double-take. The whole space has become completely filled with aggression.**

I find it interesting that there are hot hells and cold hells. If you know what it's like to be consumed by hatred and rage, you know that there's hot rage and there's cold rage.

All-consuming hatred is considered the most intense suffering of all. It feels impossible to escape because the more rage you feel, the more everything enrages you. There's never a cooling-off period because the whole thing keeps escalating.

The basic statement is "You're against me." You see the outer world and environment as an enemy.

Q&A

Q: I think of the hungry ghost realm in terms of addictions. Can you talk about how the two connect?

PEMA: When a person's addiction is all-consuming, they probably cycle through all or most of the realms. For instance, getting high on drugs is essentially a god-realm experience that lasts a short time. You crave that experience and keep trying to recreate it. But then it gets harder and harder to get high, so you have to take more and more drugs. Constantly comparing your mundane experience with being high is like the jealous gods always comparing themselves to the gods. Then, if whatever you're addicted to—food, heroin, sex—takes over your life, you get into the hell experience. Your world turns against you and becomes your enemy. The hungry ghost aspect of addiction is wanting more and more, never getting enough.

Many people have described addiction to me as feeling like you're trapped in a realm. For instance, with an eating disorder, there's nothing happening except wanting to eat or wanting not to eat. This is also true with addiction to drugs or sex. There's nothing else happening. It can even occur with more mundane obsessions or preoccupations, such as being totally consumed in your career or in looking for a place to live.

We can get really stuck. The key to escaping a realm is not to struggle but to stay present, feeling what we feel with kindness. We're all addicted in one way or another, and if the addiction is strong, we have to go through detox. But what Rinpoche's talking about is more than detox. He is presenting a way to connect with natural openness.

Samsara is made up of six realms of addicts. We sentient beings are addicted, bodhisattvas are recovering, and buddhas are recovered—permanently.

Q: I know a student of Buddhism who has no desire to put himself in others' shoes. The idea of "May someone be happy and full of peace" or even "May they understand suffering and the root of suffering, and happiness and the root of happiness" doesn't resonate with him at all. What resonates with him is "May you have your experience." I can't decide whether that's really enlightened or really callous. What can I say to help him open up to the possibility of feeling compassion and seeing it as necessary?

PEMA: I would say, yes, have your experience, fully and completely. Then you'll naturally understand, without any effort, what other people go through because your experience of pain is the same experience as everybody else's. When you get burned, fire feels the same to you as it does to anybody else. When someone you love betrays you or dies, the way that hurts is the same with any human being of any culture on the planet. Anguish and grief and joy feel the same in the heart.

I would say go that way fully, but not just as another form of spiritual materialism. You can't only "have your experience" when it's comfortable or exciting. You have to include "bad" experience. You could say, "Have your experience when you have a toothache. Have your experience when you have insomnia, when you're lonely, when you're angry. Then you'll understand what people go through and why they act the way they do."

THREE

SITTING MEDITATION

THE FOOL

THIS CHAPTER ON the practice of meditation has five sections: "The Fool," "Simplicity," "Mindfulness and Awareness," "Boredom," and "The Way of the Buddha." Rinpoche begins the chapter with a question. Having been introduced to ego and our neuroses in all their six realms' manifestations, **what do we do now?**

I remember feeling very encouraged by his answer: **We have to relate with our mental gossip and our emotions simply and directly, without philosophy. We have to use the existing material, which is ego's hang-ups and credentials and deceptions, as a starting point.** I felt if this is the case, then I have plenty of material to work with. How wonderful! We could meet ourselves as we are and, as he used to say, not be "afraid to be a fool."

Rinpoche stressed surrendering our attempts to become a better ego, a more evolved person. All the other spiritual traditions I explored at that time were oriented toward "transcending" and somehow leaving all the messy stuff behind. For me, that just didn't work. I would have loved to transcend my unhappiness, anger, and resentment, but I could never get the knack of it. Rinpoche's teachings were the first that spoke to me about what I was going through. Believe me, it was a big relief.

Rinpoche's way of guiding us was, at that time, unique in the West. Although sitting meditation was common to the Zen and Theravada traditions, it was not taught at all in the Tibetan Buddhist tradition. If you went to any other Tibetan lama, you learned traditional compassion practices that involved visualization and mantras, but not sitting meditation or walking meditation. Simple, uncluttered meditation was what I badly needed. I needed to get a close look at my habitual patterns and reactivity and make friends with all of it.

In this chapter, when Rinpoche said we were **on the kindergarten level** when it came to knowing ourselves, I resonated with that. When he said that we needed to **acknowledge that we are fools** and start from there, I resonated with that. (I understood "fool" to mean that we had a lot to learn.) I was magnetized by his message that **if we can accept our imperfections as they are, quite ordinarily, then we can use them as part of the path**. This was a path of nonrejection, a path of unconditional acceptance, not a path of getting rid of our imperfections and making them into enemies. This was a path that made sense to me, and I've been on it ever since.

SIMPLICITY

"SIMPLICITY" HERE refers to the meditation technique. It means the bare minimum. It also has the sense of being without cultural trappings.

Thoughts, in the technique that Rinpoche taught us, were recognized simply as "thoughts," a neutral term without bias. We begin **to see thoughts as simple phenomena, no matter whether they are pious thoughts or evil thoughts, domestic thoughts, whatever they may be. One does not relate to them as belonging to a particular category, as being good or bad; just see them as simple thoughts.**

Rinpoche begins this section by saying, **Meditation practice is based on dropping dualistic fixation. . . .** That's quite an astounding statement: Dualism, the fundamental sense of me and other—the fundamental cause of our suffering—can be dropped. He explains how to do this in simple terms—maybe not so simple to do but simple to understand. We drop dualistic fixation by **dropping the struggle of good against bad**. In terms of sitting meditation, this means letting our thoughts and emotions be just as they are without labeling them as positive or negative.

Rinpoche presented meditation as a way to experience for ourselves that our thoughts are not all that solid. When we believe them, they seem solid and real; but when we don't, we see how wispy they are, how **transparent**. It's like the bumper sticker that says "Don't believe everything you think." Meditation is a way to get a wider perspective on our irritations and complaints, our hopes and fears: **If one is able to see ego from an aerial point of view, then one is able to see its humorous quality.**

Rather than being something to destroy, ego is something to become very familiar with—not familiar in the "grin and bear it," grit-your-teeth style but familiar with a sense of humor, with warmth and even appreciation. If we take thoughts too seriously, which we usually do for sure, we are actually feeding them. **Thoughts,** as he puts it, **need your attention to survive.** My insight into this, after over forty years of meditation, is extremely simple: When we don't feed them, thoughts fade away. But when a few words become a paragraph, and that paragraph becomes a chapter, our thoughts become overwhelming and begin to control our lives.

The statement in *The Myth of Freedom* that completely caught me by surprise and shifted how I viewed spiritual practice altogether was that meditation is **not an attempt to achieve happiness, nor is it the attempt to achieve mental calm or peace, though they could be by-products of meditation**. Until then, I'd thought the whole idea was to be calm and peaceful, which was discouraging because it was so far from my current experience. The first time I received meditation instruction at one of Rinpoche's centers, the San Francisco Dharmadhatu, the instructor told me right off that **meditation should not be regarded as a vacation from irritation**. I found these words refreshing; they gave me the feeling that I had come to the right place. (To my amusement, as it turns out, her words were a direct quote from this section of the book.)

Some people were put off by looking at the spiritual path this way. They were not interested in a practice that brought their habitual patterns and negative propensities out into the open so they could see them. I remember once giving a man meditation instruction at the Buddhist center where I was living. After practicing the simple technique faithfully for one or two days, he announced angrily that "it didn't work." When asked exactly what he meant, he said, "When you practice meditation, you're supposed to experience bliss and deep well-being, and all I experienced was a lot of highly disturbing mental chatter."

Rinpoche's encouragement in this section to **try to become the technique** eluded me for a long time. Instead of watching the breath, we were instructed to become "one with" the breath. I had no idea how to do that or even what it meant. Then one of my meditation instructors told me to "feel the breath" as it goes out—not to watch it but to *feel* it. With this advice, something clicked. As Rinpoche says, the technique is not a **profound ceremony of some kind** but just **a simple process, extremely simple**.

In general, the sitting meditation in all Buddhist traditions is very simple, very basic. There's an object of meditation that you keep coming back to. Whenever your mind wanders off, no big deal. Just come back to the object, with no judgment. Just keep it simple, the bare minimum.

Interestingly, simplicity is also a description of the fruition of meditation. It's not only the path; simplicity is a description of how you perceive reality when you're completely present, when you're receptive and not struggling, not filling the space with your interpretations, preconceptions, or opinions. There's a sense of complete simplicity. Even in the midst of chaos and noise, there's a sense of simplicity.

MINDFULNESS AND AWARENESS

MINDFULNESS AND awareness are two fundamental qualities of mind—everyone's mind, not just meditators. The word *mindfulness* points to the ability to stay present, to be precise and right here, to be "on the dot," as Rinpoche would say.

Unfortunately, most of the human species has been training for years (probably lifetimes) in being distracted. We've become experts at this. Effortlessly our thoughts go on and on, and we go on and on with them. This is what we notice first when we start meditating: We are rarely present and are easily carried away by thoughts and emotions. If you have even mild attention deficit disorder (ADD), you may feel that your mind definitely, absolutely, without question, does *not* have the innate ability to stay on—or anywhere near—the dot. Honestly, in this age of smartphones and social media, when it's a challenge not to be distracted, many of us might question this teaching about our innate mindfulness.

However, accept this good news: Even the most active mind really does have a natural capacity to stay present. Meditation allows us to return to the state where this capacity can begin functioning again. The simple technique of returning again and again to an object of meditation is designed to tame our wild and restless mind.

Over and over again, without harshness or criticism, we bring the mind back to the breath, to sound, to our body sensations—to whatever object we are using at that time. We tame the mind like a horse whisperer would tame a beautiful wild horse—with gentleness, but also precision. It's very repetitive, and it does the job.

This is also true of mindfulness in everyday life. We simply come back to brushing our teeth, to washing the dishes, to opening the computer. We can use anything to bring back the wandering mind. When your phone rings, wait for two or three rings, come back to being right here, and then pick up. Simple practices like this uncover the amazing ability of the mind to stay present.

Mindfulness is the process of relating with individual situations directly, precisely, definitely. You communicate or connect with problematic situations or irritating situations in a simple way. . . . They are conditioned situations (meaning they are born and pass away) **but they could be seen accurately and precisely by the unconditioned mindfulness.**

Rinpoche compares mindfulness to a microscope, whose **function . . . is just to clearly present what is there. Mindfulness need not refer to the past or the future; it is fully in the now.**

Awareness, sometimes called "presently knowing," is the mind's innate capacity to know what's happening. It's the connecting-the-dots quality of mind. This is the aspect of mind that knows when it's present and when it's wandering. The Buddha taught a simple meditation where you say,

"Breathing in, I know I am breathing in. Breathing out, I know I am breathing out." That's an example of awareness, the knowing quality of mind.

When you meditate for an extended period, you can get so lost in thought that you write whole novels, operas, computer programs. Yet at some point, mind just comes back. All by itself, without any effort on your part, mind simply wakes up and is present. It's awareness that recognizes mind has been gone, and awareness that recognizes it's back.

Rinpoche, however, described the function of awareness slightly differently. He described it as providing room, providing space, like **giving a huge, luscious meadow to a restless cow**. There's restlessness and the space in which restlessness occurs, the environment in which it occurs. Being mindful of the restlessness—being right with it—and having the spaciousness of awareness allow the cow to relax. **The cow might be restless for a while in its huge meadow, but at some stage, because there is so much space, the restlessness becomes irrelevant. So the cow eats and eats and eats and relaxes and falls asleep.**

Elsewhere, Rinpoche said that when the mind is spacious and open, our thoughts and emotions are like little bugs that keep flying around but can't find anywhere to land. With that much space, the thoughts and emotions lose their glue.

Mindfulness as a practice can be quite uptight and self-conscious, but when combined with the expansiveness of awareness, the tendency to get too immersed in the details is softened and given lots of space. Mind becomes tamed through both precision and awareness, through bringing out both the on-the-dot quality and the spacious, nonjudgmental, knowing quality of mind.

These teachings laid the groundwork for later teachings where Rinpoche put special emphasis on meditation in action. As he says here, **Mindfulness and awareness work together to bring acceptance of living situations as they are.** Just your ordinary living situation, with all its seeming mundaneness, when mixed with the precision of mindfulness and the unbiased, spacious knowing of awareness, becomes a vehicle for awakening.

BOREDOM

IN THE EARLY seventies, when I first entered Rinpoche's sangha, then called Vajradhatu, there were many phrases that I heard all the time. Two of them are presented in this section: "an operation without anesthetic" and "cool boredom."

Sitting meditation, Rinpoche taught, could be compared to undergoing an operation, an operation to remove our credentials, our rather big-deal sense of being an important person—or even an unimportant person. The operation was to cut through spiritual materialism and enable us to let go of holding on to ourselves. But it had to be an operation without anesthesia, **like natural childbirth**, as he says in this section. We needed to be fully present with our ignorance, our aggression, our restlessness—fully present no matter what, with whatever occurred. With the accuracy of mindfulness and the awake, spacious quality of awareness, we would find nowhere to hide. At least that was the idea.

Once when I was a meditation instructor for a *dathün*, a monthlong meditation retreat, I got a good look at how creative my students could be in finding ways to anesthetize themselves. They certainly looked like they were meditating—good posture, proper eye gaze—but one person reported listening to music in his head all day long, and another said she spent her time on the meditation cushion designing a house.

When I asked one man how he was doing, he said, "Great!" He was able to entertain himself with his thoughts for hours, so he was having a thoroughly good time.

These examples gave me a deeper appreciation of the fact that the operation without anesthesia required a commitment to following the instructions. Of course mind wanders off, but when it comes back, for the operation to be successful, we need to return to the breath, not continue entertaining and distracting ourselves.

This is where Rinpoche's praise for boredom comes in. When doing the practice as instructed, without anesthesia, boredom is inevitable. The practice can be exciting at the beginning, but after the honeymoon period, the excitement wears itself out. As Rinpoche says, you start thinking, **"I'm supposed to get something out of Buddhism and meditation. I'm supposed to attain different levels of realization. I haven't. I'm bored stiff."**

All the credential quality has worn itself out. It isn't that much fun anymore. This is the stage of what Rinpoche calls "hot boredom," and it's an important milestone for the practitioner. Experiencing restless, agitated boredom is a sign that our practice is deepening. **Boredom is important because boredom is anti-credential. Credentials are entertaining, always bringing you something new, something lively, something fantastic, all kinds of solutions. When you take away the idea of credentials, then there is boredom.** Boredom, Rinpoche taught, is an **undoing process**, an undoing of ego's attempt to avoid the nitty-gritty of the present moment.

We were encouraged to not run away from boredom, to appreciate it until it became **cool boredom, like a mountain**

river. *Cool boredom* became a popular term, but I question whether very many of us knew what it meant. We sure knew what hot boredom meant, but sitting without struggling against it was like a koan. How in the world to do that? For me, at least, it was challenging.

The way I finally understood cool boredom was not on the meditation cushion, as one might expect. I tasted it fully when I was visiting my aging mother in Mexico. She spent all day inside with the curtains drawn, and I felt she would really appreciate it if I stayed with her. But this was warm, sunny, vibrant, full-of-life Mexico, and I almost couldn't bear staying put in that dark room. I was so restless, bored, and unhappy that I literally thought I was going to smash the door down. It was no-escape hot boredom—big time.

But I had traveled a long way, and she wanted my company and wanted to talk, so what to do? It was choiceless. I could continue to struggle and make myself even more miserable, or I could settle down with Mom and just be there as wholeheartedly as possible. Once I committed to staying, I began to calm down. The struggle was over. I wasn't going anywhere but right here with my dear old mom.

People would come in and visit for a while, and I enjoyed that. The light would shift, the shadows would change, and we'd have a meal and then chat some more or just sit there quietly, and it all became just fine. I didn't have the urge to bolt. I didn't obsess about "When will this end?" I felt at ease. This was when I finally experienced **cool boredom, like a mountain river.**

As Rinpoche writes, **It flows and flows and flows, methodically and repetitiously, but it is very cooling, very refreshing. Mountains never get tired of being mountains**

and waterfalls never get tired of being waterfalls. . . . It is a good feeling to be bored, constantly sitting and sitting. The key, I found, was not to squirm and wiggle and distract myself but just commit to being there, fully and completely—no exits.

THE WAY OF THE BUDDHA

THE MEDITATION technique that Rinpoche taught is referred to as *shamatha-vipashyana*. Like mindfulness, shamatha provides precision—being precisely where we are rather than daydreaming. In this section, he introduces vipashyana as that which connects us with a larger environment.

The way he presents vipashyana here is similar to the way he talks about awareness in the context of mindfulness and awareness. As he writes, **Breath is the object of meditation** (that's the shamatha aspect), **but the environment around the breath is also part of the meditative situation** (that's the vipashyana aspect).

Once I heard Rinpoche explain how shamatha without vipashyana could become credential-oriented. He said it would be closer to a goal-oriented concentration (something he discouraged) than to authentic shamatha-vipashyana. With shamatha-vipashyana meditation, you don't get so focused on following the breath that you are easily startled. I once saw a meditator almost leap right off his cushion when he was gently touched on the shoulder. Not only that, he let out a piercing yelp. Because vipashyana allows for openness to the environment, if there's a loud noise or someone touches your shoulder, you notice, of course, but you aren't startled. At least most of the time.

In shamatha-vipashyana practice, we keep our eyes open because we're not trying to block out what's happening around us. Sometimes when I sit with students before a teaching, people are still coming in and walking to their seats. You might imagine that this would be distracting, but in this style of meditation, you don't consider "distractions" to be distractions. If your mind wanders, you just come back to being present without any big deal. This prepares you for anything that might come along. Keeping our eyes open brings an awareness of the space in which we are meditating, the space in which we are returning to the object of meditation.

Vipashyana, as Rinpoche explains, literally means "insight." It can also be translated as "superior seeing"—the seeing that comes from direct meditative experience. In the way it is most widely taught, such as at the Insight Meditation Society or in the tradition of S. N. Goenka, vipashyana involves meditation on an object or activity, such as the breath, sense perceptions, thoughts, walking, or eating. However, Rinpoche taught vipashyana quite differently, as the open, expansive quality of mind. As he writes, **Insight is relating not only with what you see but also with the implications of it, the totality of the space and objects around it.**

To experience vipashyana, he said, we don't need to change our meditation technique. Vipashyana evolves by itself, gradually, as our sense of space begins to expand. This is close to how Dzigar Kongtrul Rinpoche explains it when he says that by calming our discursive mind through shamatha, vipashyana will slowly dawn and we will "see the nature of reality, which is something we do not normally see or experience."

When Rinpoche emphasizes vipashyana as an experience of expansiveness, he refers again to the grain-of-sand analogy. He says that we could follow the way of the Buddha, who, like **a grain of sand living in the vast desert**, has no sense of personal territory, no need to struggle and battle, no need to cling and grasp. There is a feeling of light-handedness and balance. With vipashyana, **the whole thing becomes more expansive, more open**. There's always something happening, and it's happening in a big space.

Rinpoche presented this way of practicing as following the way of the Buddha, the way of passionlessness, the way of nongrasping, the way of nonaggression. The **vipashyana perspective,** he writes here, **is a panoramic situation in which you can come and go freely and your relationship with the world is open. It is the ultimate nonviolence.**

FOUR

WORKING WITH THE EMOTIONS

THE DUALISTIC BARRIER

Of all Rinpoche's teachings, the material in this chapter, "Working with the Emotions," has had the biggest influence on me. Its three sections—"The Dualistic Barrier," "Lion's Roar," and "Working with Negativity"—are packed with potentially life-changing advice. At least, that's how they have affected me.

Rinpoche begins "The Dualistic Barrier" by going deeper into the topic of spiritual materialism. If we experience cool boredom or other signs of "good" practice, **we must look further at the desire for credentials**, he says, declaring that we can use even these positive signs to create **a sense of comfort, a sense of security**—in both our sitting meditation and in everyday life. As he writes in *Cutting Through Spiritual Materialism*, "The problem is that ego can convert anything to its own use, even spirituality."

He gives the example of someone who has just finished a comfortable **ideal sitting meditation period**, where they are very proud of themselves. Finally they got it right. I remember being at a teaching where someone raised their hand and said, "I labeled every thought, and by the end I was with every breath." Rinpoche answered, not unkindly but with an incredulous look on his face, "So what?"

In the situation Rinpoche describes here, after your **ideal sitting**, you go to make a phone call, only to discover that the phone has been cut off, so you get enraged and fly off the handle. **Little things like that happen all the time,** he writes. **If we experience such situations, then we begin to realize that our practice is credential-oriented, that there is a belief in some kind of basic harmony.**

In chapter 1, Rinpoche described how our preference for harmony is a significant cause of dissatisfaction. This belief that we could achieve an ideal balanced harmonious state goes very deep. Rinpoche advocates a more realistic approach to life. It's not helpful to boycott whole parts of life because they are uncomfortable. As he said in the "Mindfulness and Awareness" section of the previous chapter, **You communicate or connect with problematic situations or irritating situations in a simple way. There is ignorance, there is restlessness, there is passion, there is aggression. They need not be praised or condemned. They are just regarded as fits.**

An example from my life is working with the emotion of pride—in particular, spiritual pride: "I'm so highly regarded. Many people have actually told me that my teachings have saved their lives." Then I go home to visit family and all my neuroses are exposed. By the second day, I'm almost continually impatient and critical. This is what Rinpoche would call an "anti-credential experience." It humbles me and shows me how far I have to go. Such **potential and unexpected disturbances** as these are the best of teachers.

As Rinpoche says, **The problems of everyday life are a way of destroying our credentials, our comfort and security, and they present us with an opportunity to relate with our emotions.** We can be quite full of ourselves, quite oblivious to our not-so-hidden habitual patterns, and then an embarrassingly dramatic meltdown pops that bubble fast.

The rest of this section is a general teaching on relating to our emotions, with which, he admits, **it is extremely difficult and quite challenging to work.** He begins with a description of emotions that I've always found immensely helpful: **When energy and thought are mixed together, they become the vivid and colorful emotions.** Over the years, I've made practical use of this insight whenever possible. When strong emotions arise, I try to experience their energy without thought as a way to defuse their power. I let go of the conversation in my head, all my versions of what's happening, and make friends with what's left—only energy, the underlying energy. I encourage you to try this and see what happens.

The reason we usually get so carried away and overwhelmed by emotions is **because our relationship to the emotions is not quite clear.** I find this to be true. My relationship with anger, for instance, used to be confusing because I feared my anger. I was embarrassed by it, and I didn't want to be seen totally losing control. Working with the instructions in this chapter is what shifted that.

The key to working with our emotions is seeing their **transparency**, which, he says, **involves removing the dualistic barriers set up by concepts.** I finally understood what he meant by "dualistic barrier" because of a relationship that had ended badly. I was holding on to painful emotions and couldn't imagine how the conflict would ever be resolved, but I knew it was really important to stay open. After a few years, I received a letter of apology from the person involved, and that was all it took. All my hard feelings evaporated. Instead I felt only tenderness and gratitude.

The sense of separation I had been feeling, the alienation I'd experienced, was a dualistic barrier. I could actually feel it as a barrier between us. This barrier was set up by the concepts I had been holding, the concepts of their "badness" and my "righteousness." When those dissolved, so did the barrier. **The barrier,** Rinpoche writes, **the wall between you and your projections, the hysterical and paranoid aspect of your relationship to your projections, has been removed—not exactly removed, but seen through.**

Seeing the transparency of emotions is more challenging than seeing the transparency of thoughts. With thoughts, at least in meditation, you can touch them lightly, as if they were a speech balloon, and let them dissolve on their own. The instruction I especially like is to touch them like a feather touching a bubble. However, if thoughts are emotionally charged, they will quickly return. But you can touch them again and they will dissolve again. You can do this patiently, over and over.

With emotions, the dissolving, the seeing through, happens more rapidly when there's a change of focus, a shift in how you're perceiving the situation. For example, a student told me how she was feeling consumed by jealousy because she was convinced that her lover was secretly seeing someone else. Then she overheard a conversation that made her realize she had been making up the whole thing. Suddenly that huge, raging, throbbing jealousy dissolved and she saw the flimsiness of the emotion. Something so solid evaporated like magic, and she was left wondering, "What was that all about?"

The way Rinpoche taught meditation supported me in seeing the transparency of my thoughts and emotions. For instance, I was not instructed to concentrate on the breath but rather to let it go out and dissolve into space. When thoughts arose, I wasn't instructed to treat them as an enemy that was destroying my perfect meditation but to take the attitude of "no big deal." This light-touch attitude helped me and many others to get the feeling of letting go.

As Rinpoche says in his *Profound Treasury of the Ocean of Dharma*, "You touch or contact the experience of actually being there, then you let go. That touch-and-go process applies to your awareness of your breath and also your awareness in day-to-day living." It applies also to your thoughts and emotions. You touch them, and you let go. Sometimes you can do this, sometimes you can't. But this is no problem. You simply go forward, continuing to touch and go.

In this section, Rinpoche distinguishes seeing from looking. He uses "seeing" to mean direct experience and "looking" to mean laying something on top of that experience. You can practice seeing at any time. Simply stop, slow down, and see. Then when you notice that seeing has become looking, you simply come back to seeing—no problem. **Actually,** he says, **we do not see things completely as they are. Generally, we perceive something, and then we look.** First we automatically see without concepts, and then we start to make a story—we "look"—and move away from the direct, uncluttered experience.

Seeing things means accepting what they are, but looking means unnecessary effort to make sure that you are safe, that nothing is going to confuse you in your relationship to the world. So we create our security by putting things into categories, naming them, by using relative terms to identify their interrelationships, how they fit together. And this security brings temporary happiness and comfort.

We could all share stories about an experience that didn't make sense until we rearranged the pieces so that it did—only to find out that the rearrangement of pieces was actually a misinterpretation. Mingyur Rinpoche tells a story about waiting in an airport and becoming paranoid because one of the officials was staring at him. He concluded that for some reason he was in big trouble. Every time he looked over, the man seemed to be more and more hostile. When the official started to walk toward him, he panicked. Then the man said, "Are you Mingyur Rinpoche? I read your book and really enjoyed it." After that, whenever Mingyur Rinpoche glanced at the official, he saw him as a warm and friendly fellow.

In how we usually work with our emotions, **there is no attempt to deal with projections as exciting and fluid situations at all; instead the world is seen as being absolutely solid and stiff.** We don't appreciate how interesting it is that situations are open-ended rather than fixed. In a later chapter, Rinpoche describes how we see a vague figure in the distance walking toward us. Initially we have a fresh, unfixed take. Then in comes our interpretation, our past conditioning and history. We label them as friend or foe, and the freshness is lost.

The solidity and stiffness we perceive has nothing to do with the outside world. On the contrary, Rinpoche says, **we are dealing here with mental solidity—harshness, a metallic quality.** Sadly, we don't then let our misperceptions be. They trigger something in us—an emotional response of like or dislike—and before we know it, we have full-blown, emotionally charged prejudices. Letting go of these strongly held beliefs isn't easy, but it's a good start to become aware of how we keep these biases alive, and to catch and question ourselves when we start going down that particular rabbit hole.

All the instructions I've given over the years on working with emotions have been highly influenced by this chapter. For instance, I often say, "Drop the storyline and go to the felt experience." Experience the energy of your emotions directly, without talking to yourself about it, and when the storyline returns—as it usually does—simply return to the naked experience.

Here Rinpoche says, **So the intelligent way of working with emotions is to try to relate with their basic substance, the abstract quality of the emotions, so to speak. The basic "isness" quality of the emotions, the fundamental nature of the emotions, is just energy. And if one is able to relate with energy, then the energies have no conflict with you.** When you don't struggle against the energy, when you don't divide yourself in two, then the barrier between you and your own emotions dissolves.

They become a natural process, he writes. **So trying to suppress or getting carried away by the emotions become irrelevant once a person is completely able to see their basic characteristic, the emotions as they are, which is shunyata.** When we fully experience the emotions without spin-off, we experience *shunyata*, or "emptiness," which Rinpoche describes as **the absence of relative concepts**. We see that the emotions can't be pinned down and that we can relate to their basic energy without biting the hook and getting swept away.

When there is no panic involved in dealing with the emotions, then you can deal with them completely, properly. Then you are like someone who is completely skilled in their profession, who does not panic, but just does their work completely, thoroughly. This is how you can relate to your emotions: Just be with the felt sense of the energy, the "isness" of the energy, completely and thoroughly without panicking. Even if you do panic, you can still be with the energy of panic.

Rinpoche points out that the spiritual path, meditation, and our relationship with life altogether are often experienced as a struggle, a battle. When ego is presented, people think of it as a villain to be expelled. However, we're not talking about destroying ego but coming to know it so well that we can relax.

Usually when we speak of spirituality, we tend to think that we are fighting the bad; we are good, spirituality is the ultimate good, the epitome of good, and the other side is bad. Well, you can see the results of this kind of thinking in every country of the world: Jews versus Muslims, Muslims versus Hindus, Protestants versus Catholics. **But true spirituality is not a battle,** he says. **It is the ultimate practice of nonviolence.**

We are not regarding any part of us as being a villain, an enemy, he says, **but we are trying to use everything as a part of the natural process of life. As soon as a notion of polarity between good and bad develops, then we are caught in spiritual materialism.**

Rinpoche is pointing here to natural, underlying openness, which is by its nature unbiased—not prejudiced and not divided. At any time, under any circumstances, we can connect with this underlying simplicity. We're not dividing ourselves against ourselves or dividing ourselves against others but working with things as they are—as they always are before bias enters the picture.

LION'S ROAR

IN "BUDDHADHARMA without Credentials," Rinpoche said two things that, at least for me, have become famous quotes. Both of them appear in this section of *The Myth of Freedom*. One is **Chaos should be regarded as extremely good news.** The other is **Whatever occurs in the samsaric mind is regarded as the path; everything is workable. It is a fearless proclamation—the lion's roar.**

When my friend was having a mental breakdown, she pinned the second quote on her wall. Seeing those words every day, she told me, was what got her through.

The lion's roar is a fearless statement based on unconditional confidence. We have no fear because there's nothing we can see about ourselves that isn't workable. When we know that to be true, without any doubt, we gain confidence in our ability to work with ourselves just as we are.

Rinpoche often used the Sanskrit word *maitri*, which translates as "loving-kindness." He emphasized having maitri toward others but also toward ourselves. Having maitri toward ourselves means having an unconditional friendship with ourselves, just as we are, with all our warts and pimples, all our weird little ways and beauty.

However, if we have challenges—if we have an addiction of some kind, or if we're always flying into a rage—there is still work to be done. This work is not about acting out or repressing. It's about having a direct, unfettered relationship with our own energies and anything we might feel—in our heart, in our stomach, in our nervous system. Whatever comes up, we could have a fearless relationship with it. We're talking about showing up for our own energy, pleasant or unpleasant. That's the lion's roar.

In this section, Rinpoche gives a five-stage process for working with emotions. This didn't go down in history as a widely used formula, but I've always found it very helpful. He came up with these five stages as a teaching device to help us connect with direct experience, to help us transmute neuroses into wisdom.

The five stages are seeing, hearing, smelling, touching, and transmuting. Most of the time, I can't remember what all five are, but I've been influenced by the overall message and quality of the teaching. The idea is to drop the storyline and go directly to the experience, the sensation of the emotion without interpretation. Then you can explore the emotion using the five-step method he describes.

Although there are five stages, I feel that they are all a way of talking about the fifth stage, transmutation, which Rinpoche compares to alchemy. It is **not a matter of rejecting the basic qualities of the emotions. Rather, as in the alchemical practice of changing lead into gold, you do not reject the basic qualities of the material, but you change its appearance and substance somewhat.**

To talk about this from a vajrayana point of view, say you have an emotion such as rage or resentment—any emotion in the category of aggressive feelings toward yourself or others. This includes any feeling of "I don't like" or "I don't want."

Whatever variation of aggression you feel, you don't try to change the energy. You don't calm it down or exaggerate it. You don't repress or act out. You simply have a direct experience of the energy. If you do this, the energy itself doesn't change, but your experience of it does.

When the energy that we call "rage" or "hatred" or "irritation" is free of fixation, you can experience what is called "mirror-like wisdom." If you're seeking wisdom, you find it right there in the neurosis, not elsewhere. This is why Rinpoche taught not getting rid of emotions. We would be throwing away our wisdom. Yet we have to go through an alchemical process before we realize this.

Another analogy that's often used is ice and water. If you are intent on finding water, but all you have is ice, you don't throw out the ice. You melt it. You don't have to look for another source of water. You find it right there in what you already have.

Wisdom and neurotic emotion are the same energy. It's wisdom when the energy remains fluid, and it's neurosis when the energy is filtered through ego and frozen into concepts, prejudices, and beliefs. Accepting the energy and staying with it is like melting ice to get water. This is how rage becomes "mirror-like wisdom," how craving becomes "discriminating-awareness wisdom," and how jealousy becomes "all-accomplishing wisdom."

Rinpoche used various methods to try to help students transform the energy of their emotions. He developed something called "maitri space awareness" and created five rooms, each with a certain shape and color. Even the windows had particular shapes.

When you entered one of these rooms, you would be instructed to get into a certain posture. The whole thing was designed so that the room and the posture would churn up a specific emotion. Then the idea was to stay with the emotion, getting to know it thoroughly. In some rooms you might feel at ease and not provoked at all. Usually one of the five would be your favorite. However, there was always at least one room that was very uncomfortable. The color and shape of the room, the window, and your posture heightened a specific emotion. This was where you spent the most time.

The five-stage process helps us **respect whatever happens to our state of mind.** The first stage, *seeing*, is having an attitude of acceptance—accepting your energy. Accepting doesn't mean applauding it, writing poems and songs about it, or justifying it. It means not rejecting the energy. If you appreciate that the energy is your wisdom, you might get very curious about staying with it.

Seeing is simply an attitude of "This is what's happening now." As Rinpoche puts it, with seeing **we accept [the emotions] as part of the pattern of mind, without question, without reference back to the scriptures, without help from credentials, but we directly acknowledge that they are so, that these things are happening.**

The second stage, *hearing*, refers to feeling the intensity of the energy, **experiencing the pulsation of such energy, the energy upsurge as it comes toward you.**

Third, *smelling*, is an attitude that the upsurging energy is workable, **as when you smell food and the smell becomes an appetizer, whetting your appetite before you eat. It smells like a good meal, it smells delicious, although you have not eaten it yet.**

Fourth, *touching*, means knowing the quality of the energy, **feeling the nitty-gritty of the whole thing . . . that**

your emotions are not particularly destructive or crazy but just an upsurge of energy, whatever form they take—aggressive, passive, or grasping. In its essence, the energy is fluid. But anyone who works this way knows that energy can feel very solid. It can feel stuck in your solar plexus or elsewhere. With the emotion of craving, for instance, if you rest with it instead of running, it can feel hot, cold, shaky, rock-hard, explosive, or tranquil. It comes in all conceivable and inconceivable flavors.

The last stage is *transmuting*, but as I've said, all five are part of the transmutation process. They are like a how-to for transforming neuroses into wisdom—for tapping into the wisdom inherent in the energy. This is not really "your" energy but the energy inherent in the air, trees, animals, flowers, humans. This energy is everywhere. You can feel it anytime, but it becomes most accessible when your emotions are heightened.

With transmuting, you completely join in with the energy; you become one with it. This is the same direction Rinpoche points to when he talks about "no exits," "no sidetracks," "stay present." Becoming "one with" is an experiential way of talking about nonduality.

To review the process without the terminology, first it begins with an attitude of acceptance. This is not the same thing as approval. It's matter-of-fact: "This is what's happening now." Second, you experience the energetic quality of the emotions, the "pulsation." Emotions, as we know, have various energetic qualities: sometimes like a volcanic eruption, sometimes like a tidal wave, sometimes like an icy plateau.

Third, you have the attitude that everything is workable. Whatever happens in your confused state of mind and confused emotions is the path to enlightenment. This is the fearless proclamation—the lion's roar.

Fourth, you regard emotions as simply an upsurge of energy. You experience their insubstantial, changing energy without internal dialogue, without labels. You know that energy and feel its texture, its **nitty-gritty**, without resistance, rejection, or acting out. Fifth and finally, you become one with the emotion. This is the process of transmutation.

Rinpoche gives a humorous description of how we try to avoid our own energy and the discomfort of our emotions by putting on "patches"—**metaphysical, philosophical, religious patches**—patches of all kinds. These are basically concepts: emotional takes, biased views, interpretations, and philosophies. We use these concepts to cover ourselves and our emotions, to withdraw, to conceal whatever it is we don't know how to deal with: **Our concern is to save face, avoid being embarrassed, avoid being challenged by our emotions.** If one patch, one philosophical interpretation or biased view, doesn't work, we apply another, and then another, until we're covered with patches. We have a zillion methods of turning away and not dealing. But, Rinpoche says, **unless one is completely mummified, which is death, being a corpse, there is no way to completely protect oneself. For a living human being, patchwork is an absolutely impractical idea.**

WORKING WITH NEGATIVITY

This section is based on the teaching that got me into Buddhism. The way I remember it is probably like a childhood memory that's not completely accurate. It was the early 1970s, and I was at the lowest part of my life, in a state of practically catatonic depression, which was juiced up by rage. These emotions were characterized by unrelenting groundlessness.

At that time, every day of the week and every place you looked, there were spiritual offerings. I went to them all trying to find answers. They say that when you really hit bottom, when you really hurt, then spiritual teachings become like food or medicine. They are no longer merely interesting. You're looking for answers to your pain.

Everything I encountered I interpreted as saying, "Look toward the good." Transcend this experience. Chant until you don't feel this way anymore. But I was at the stage where all these things only made it worse. Chanting made it worse. Smoking marijuana made it worse. Going to a movie made it worse. Trying to distract myself in any way made it worse.

One day, I walked out of the school where I was teaching and saw, on the front seat of my friend's pickup truck, a copy of *Garuda* magazine. This was a publication that Rinpoche's students put together in the early days. I had never heard of Rinpoche, and I didn't know Buddhism from Hinduism from Christianity from Islam.

The magazine was opened to an article titled "Working with Negativity." The first sentences stopped my mind: "We experience negativity as something terribly unpleasant and something we want to get rid of, something that smells foul."

I was already nodding my head. I understood this feeling of not wanting things to be how they are, not wanting the events to have happened, not wanting to be suffering so intensely. And then came the lines: "But if we look into its details, it has a very juicy smell and a very living quality. So negativity is not bad *per se*, but something living and precise, connected with reality."

Those lines were like a thunderbolt for me because I knew, somehow, that they were absolutely true and had something important to teach me. I had already been sensing that the groundlessness I felt was trying to show me something. I somehow understood that I'd discovered something that had been obscured by my ordinary routine life, by "life as usual." The ground had fallen out and given me a chance to see my life with new eyes. Yet until I came across this teaching by Rinpoche, I hadn't found anything to support my intuition. I hadn't even articulated it to myself. So once I read "something living and precise, connected with reality," I read the rest of the article like a starving person finally eating food.

When I read the article now, especially when Rinpoche gets into topics like the "four karmas," I realize I couldn't have had a clue what most of it meant because I barely have a clue what it means now. Nevertheless, I was completely captivated and blown away by the basic message.

The main part I remember reading was that there's nothing wrong with negativity. We've already established here that negativity is just our basic energy occurring in the form of "I don't like this," "I don't want this," "I want this to go away." Rinpoche said there's nothing wrong with our basic energy manifesting in these ways: as the rage, suffering, groundlessness, and depression I was feeling. The problem, he said, is "negative negativity," "double negativity," or "conceptualized negativity"—what nowadays I refer to as "the spin-off."

The *Garuda* article says, "Even in the realization of enlightenment, if we may be so presumptuous to speak of it, we would see that reality is exactly the same—simple, raw, and rugged. And so is negativity."

The direct experience—without our interpretations, without our hopes and fears—is not even the doorway or the path to enlightenment. It is a glimpse of enlightenment right now. This is like a pep talk for how you might relate the next time you are going under. Go back and read this section.

In *The Myth of Freedom*, he says, **Negativity breeds tension, friction, gossip, discontentment, but it is also very accurate, deliberate, and profound.** The problem is the conceptual overlay, the disaster scenarios and other stories, the **rationales we use to justify avoiding our pain**.

He names two rationales in particular. One is that you justify yourself—say, for being angry or hating someone, or for your dogmatic or prejudiced view. The other is that you feel ashamed of yourself. You feel bad about your emotionality. Not only that, but you fear it. Either you buy into it and say it's good, or you reject it and say it's bad.

I find this teaching on negative negativity to be so helpful. It's the teaching behind my instruction to "drop the storyline and stay with the experience." Stay with the direct, raw experience of the energy without what the meditation teacher Sharon Salzberg calls "add-ons."

In "Buddhadharma without Credentials," Rinpoche answers a student's question about depression. The student refers to depression as "a negative energy, or absence of energy."

Rinpoche's reply is so interesting to me that I will quote it at length.

> Depression is one of the very powerful energies, one of the most common energies that we have. It *is* energy. Depression is like an oxygen tank that wants to burst but is still bottled. It is a fantastic bank of energies, much more so than aggression and passion which are kind of developed and then let out. They are in some sense frivolous, whereas depression is the most dignified energy of all. . . .
>
> Try to relate to the texture of the energy in the depression situation. Depression is not just a blank, it has all kinds of intelligent things happening within it. [It] is extraordinarily interesting and a highly *intelligent* state of being. That is why you are depressed. Depression is an unsatisfied state of mind in which you feel that you have no outlet. So work with the dissatisfaction of that depression. Whatever is in it is extraordinarily powerful. It has all kinds of answers in it, but the answers are hidden. So, in fact, I think depression is one of the most powerful of all energies. It is extraordinarily *awake* energy, although you might feel sleepy.

To work with negativity, the first thing to know is that **the negative negativity must be cut through**. When you cut through it quickly and abruptly, you can have a direct, sudden experience of reality—also known as our old friend shunyata—an experience that can't be described or pinned down. The emotion is just what it is, empty of fixed ideas and labels. What cuts through the negative negativity is **the sharp blow of basic intelligence—*prajnaparamita*,** a Sanskrit word that is sometimes described as that which sees the empty nature of all things—that which sees things just as they are.

Rinpoche says that it's necessary to stop the storyline on the spot—to stop going on and on and on, and create a gap. Sometimes you can create that gap by pausing. Say you're walking along, your thoughts and emotions escalating, blind to the outer world because you're so caught up in your drama. Then it occurs to you to stop, to pause and look out, and you have a moment of direct experience: direct experience of trees or buildings, direct experience of sounds, direct experience of what Rinpoche called "nowness."

When you pause or cut through abruptly, you are "poking holes in the clouds," another of Rinpoche's expressions. The next step is just to go on with your life. As he would put it, you "disown" the direct experience and just continue whatever you're doing. Don't make the experience into *something*, into *my* experience. In other words, don't hang on to it. You have a short moment of direct experience, a direct experience of shunyata, and then you just go on with your life.

Rinpoche also warns that abruptly interrupting an emotion tends to be painful. Whether you manage to nip your anger or craving in the bud or you cut short your emotional reaction and go take a walk, the idea is to change the channel to give yourself space and bring some wisdom into the equation. You connect with your own wisdom instead of being clouded by your emotional reactivity. But when you interrupt an emotion, you're going to feel pain. Because you're not following your habitual response, you can expect to go through a kind of detox, which is very uncomfortable.

He talks about the cause of this pain and discomfort in the context of "frivolousness," a term that **refers to the extra and unnecessary mental and physical acts with which we keep ourselves busy in order not to see what actually is happening in a situation.**

He says, **It is obvious that, when you are really squashing frivolousness, you will feel pain, because there is a certain attraction toward the occupation of being frivolous. By squashing it you are completely taking away that occupation. You begin to feel that you have nothing to hold on to anymore, which is rather frightening as well as painful. What do you do then, after you have extinguished everything? Then you must not live on your heroism, on having achieved something, but just dance with the continuing process of energy that has been liberated by this destruction.** How to dance with the energy isn't always clear, but you are highly motivated to learn.

Following this discussion, Rinpoche briefly gives yet another way of working with emotions by presenting the four karmas, or four actions: pacifying, enriching, magnetizing, and destroying. The first strategy for working with emotions is pacifying. You calm them with gentleness and kindness. If that doesn't work, you try enriching, and then magnetizing. If all else fails, you destroy—abruptly, quickly, you cut through the negativity.

The first three karmas—pacifying, enriching, and magnetizing—are gentle and have more of the quality of ordinary compassion. They are the basis of being able to perform the fourth karma of destroying. In order to destroy, we first have to make friends with ourselves. Without maitri, or loving-kindness, toward ourselves, the abrupt cutting is usually not an act of love or self-compassion. It's an act of self-aggression. Instead of cutting through the unnecessary layer of negativity, we attack ourselves. Some people describe their meditation as like a battle, like having a little sergeant sitting on their shoulder. When a thought arises, instead of simply touching it and letting it go, they say, "Bad!" as if shooting down a clay pigeon. It's an attitude of struggle, self-judgment, striving to get it right.

For this reason, it's important to begin with pacifying, which is similar to what Rinpoche referred to earlier in this chapter as "seeing." It's a feeling of "This is what's happening" and accepting it. Pacifying alone may be enough; there may be no need to continue with the other three karmas. By not pushing away or rejecting it, the blocked or frozen energy could melt and start to flow naturally, all by itself.

If that doesn't happen, you apply the next karma: enriching. This means not poverty-tripping yourself. You connect with a basic sense of richness, the sense that you are basically good. Your rage, jealousy, addiction, and other neuroses are adventitious, removable. But not only that, they contain wisdom.

The karma of magnetizing comes next. This involves rousing your confidence, having the sense that you can uplift yourself instead of spiraling down. When my grandson Pete was little, he used to have frequent meltdowns. One Halloween, he had a Batman costume that had muscles. He was a skinny little guy, and when he put on that costume, he started strutting around with a sense of confidence. All of a sudden, his posture became uplifted, and he felt strong and self-assured.

Another time, we were sitting at the breakfast table, and he was on the verge of melting down about some injustice he was forced to endure. His lip was trembling, and I could see what was coming next. I knew that he loved *Star Wars*, so I asked, "Pete, what would Obi-Wan Kenobi do right now?" All of a sudden, he paused his meltdown and sat up tall. But after a few moments, his self-pitying thoughts returned. He slumped down over the table and talked himself back into feeling wronged. But when I reminded him a second time of Obi-Wan Kenobi, he roused himself completely.

That's the idea of magnetizing. You connect with your ability to cut the momentum of your reactive mind and stay with the energy. You rouse confidence that you can avoid the habitual response. You refuse to continue your "nostalgia for samsara," as Rinpoche would say. You don't have to go back to the trembling lip, the hunched posture, the getting in bed and putting the covers over your head—or whatever your style is. You don't have to throw things or scream.

Often it's more like we're magnetizing pain. We invite the thoughts to come back, we chew on them and eat them as if they're delicious food, and we just stay miserable. This is not just any old pain but our familiar type of pain, the way that we always exit when we're unhappy. Instead of going into all of that again, we rouse our confidence with the karma of magnetizing.

If these three more gentle and conventional notions of compassionate action don't work, then we perform the fourth karma of destroying.

Rinpoche says, **These four karmas are very pertinent to the process of dealing with negativity and so-called problems. First pacify, then enrich, then magnetize, and if that does not work, finally extinguish, destroy altogether. This last is necessary only when the negative negativity uses a strong pseudo-logic or a pseudo-philosophical attitude or conceptualization . . . when one is using logic and ways of justifying oneself so that situations become very heavy and very solid. We know this heaviness is taking place, but simultaneously we play tricks on ourselves, feeling that we enjoy the heaviness.**

Say you have a meltdown like Pete's. Then you connect to your basic confidence, to a feeling of inner strength. There's a sense of having applied the first three karmas. But then you start going down again. You can see yourself talking yourself back into feeling miserable. At that point, cutting the thought process abruptly and staying with the nakedness of the energy might be all that works. It might be the ultimate kindness to yourself.

In the beginning, it's better to err on the side of gentleness and work with touching the thoughts and letting them go. Err on the side of accepting all parts of yourself until you feel that the basis of loving-kindness is strong enough that you can take the next step. But in some cases, destroying may be the only thing that works. You realize that you're poisoning yourself with an old habitual pattern that has an enormous pull on you, and you say to yourself, "Stop. Just stop. I'm not going down that road again." Rinpoche called that "The Big No."

Finally, I want to go over what Rinpoche has to say about frivolousness and spontaneity. Recently I was watching a documentary in which a man was being interrogated. He was trying to hold his seat and stay calm, knowing that if he got enraged he'd make things much worse. Everything in his body language shows that he's on the verge of losing it and lashing out, giving in to his habitual pattern. You can see his hands clenching and his jaw getting stiff. But because his situation is so dangerous, his wisdom and intelligence are stronger than his habitual emotional response, and he holds his seat.

Rinpoche's instruction for dealing with provocative situations reminds me of this. He says, **You must not make an impulsive move into any situation**—particularly an emotionally charged situation. Stay with the energy and don't let it spin off into negative negativity. When something triggers you, don't be like dry grass: Someone throws a match, and you burst into flames. Instead, learn to contain the energy.

Let the situation come, then look at it, chew it properly, digest it, sit on it. The man in the documentary was doing just this. His impulse was to strike back, but he knew better, so he just had to work with the energy that was getting activated. "Look at it, chew it properly," and so on, is similar to what we talked about in the last section, with seeing, hearing, smelling, touching, and transmuting emotions.

Rinpoche goes on: **The sudden move is unhealthy, impulsive, and frivolous. Spontaneity sees situations as they are. You see, there is a difference between spontaneity and frivolousness, a very thin line dividing them. Whenever there is an impulse to do something, you should not just do it; you should work with the impulse. If you are working with it, then you will not act frivolously; you want really to see it and taste it properly, devoid of frivolousness. Frivo-**

lousness means reacting according to reflex. Frivolousness is just knee-jerk reaction, acting according to impulse. **You throw something and when it bounces back you react.**

On the other hand, Rinpoche says, **spontaneity is when you throw something and watch it and work with the energy when it bounces back at you.** This is an important distinction. It's just semantics, but he chose to use "frivolousness" to mean impulsively acting out. "Spontaneity," which he later calls "dancing" with the situation, means you don't immediately act but you experience the energy completely. At the same time, you are there, fully open to the person or situation that's triggering you but without caving in.

Q&A

Q: When you were discussing the four karmas, I read it as a way of engaging with your own experience but also with situations. You can use them if a situation is going in a harmful direction. But you mentioned that we might want to reserve that until we were further along the path, and you implied that there might be some pitfalls.

PEMA: Only destroying, the fourth karma, has pitfalls. If you're talking to someone who's all worked up and you try to pacify the situation, or help them connect with their richness, or help them feel confidence in their basic ability—their buddha nature or basic goodness—none of that is a problem. But destroying is one that people could definitely abuse.

Sometimes destroying happens naturally and is clearly a compassionate act, such as grabbing a child to stop them from running into traffic. They might start crying because they don't realize the context. It can feel abrupt and harsh, but the intention is compassionate. But this is the kind of teaching that someone could really misinterpret. For instance, Rinpoche talks about saying "Out!" when someone is being frivolous, but you can see how one might abuse that instruction.

If you had no question in your mind that destroying was an act of compassion, sure you could do it. But there have been times when I've had no doubt that I was acting abruptly out of love for somebody, and it didn't come across quite right. I once hurt someone badly because I didn't have enough skill or compassion to cut abruptly. I wasn't acting out of anger, yet I could feel there was something fishy in it. Unfortunately, I didn't realize that until I had acted. This is how we learn. We experiment with how to help, and it might succeed and it might not. Then, older but wiser, we go forward with our intention to be of help, learning as we go and often learning the hard way.

FIVE

MEDITATION IN ACTION

WORK

TAIL OF THE TIGER (now Karmê Chöling) in Barnet, Vermont, was Rinpoche's first center in the United States. In the early 1970s, the students there came up with the idea of having a seminar called "Work, Sex, and Money." Interestingly enough, Rinpoche went for it. "Work" and "Love," the first two sections of this chapter, come from that seminar.

The overall topic of this chapter, "Meditation in Action," expands on a familiar theme: Formal meditation is extremely important, but it's equally important to take this meditation into our everyday life situations. We could, as Rinpoche says, connect at all times and in all situations with **the openness of a continual meditative state**.

What allowed me to get an experiential sense, a felt sense, of what this phrase really means was Rinpoche's living example of residing fully in the present, in an ongoing state of nowness. Because of him, I came to realize that connecting with this open state of mind ongoingly, or even for **a fraction-of-a-second flash**, is a matter of contacting the atmosphere of a situation, the quality of a situation.

Rinpoche frequently urged us to become aware of the space around all that we do, the space around our thoughts and emotions, the spaciousness available at all times, in all situations. His Holiness Dilgo Khyentse Rinpoche suggested that when we become totally engulfed by the speed and pressures of life, we could go to a window and look up at the sky. This is the same idea. Getting in the habit of pausing, of stopping and allowing a gap, gives us the chance to connect with the atmosphere of the moment, the timelessness of the moment, the openness of a continual meditative state.

If you've had even a glimpse of this spaciousness during meditation, that firsthand experience will make it far easier for you to contact and recognize the **vast energy of openness** at any time. While sitting formally or doing anything else—at work, at home, alone, or with others—all situations present opportunities for awakening from the bubble of ego and experiencing life freshly.

In terms of work, Rinpoche begins by presenting two pitfalls, two attitudes that could keep your work from being a vehicle for awakening. The first is being a workaholic, where you use work to avoid being present. He gives the example of a person who, whenever they feel depressed, afraid, insecure, or edgy in any way, immediately starts polishing a table. Today, we pick up our phones to check our messages or scroll through social media. We don't allow any space in our life. The greatest challenge that we have these days is the speed at which things are happening and the amount of seduction there is to fill up every moment. Rinpoche refers to this as **seek[ing] a kind of pleasure of the moment**.

The second pitfall is an attitude prevalent in the counterculture at the time Rinpoche gave these teachings: **regarding working as something to revolt against**. This, he says, includes looking down on people with conventional lives instead of understanding that everyone has a lot to teach us.

Rinpoche's message, which was revolutionary then and is revolutionary now, was to join in. Rather than stand back and judge, we can join the party. Once when I was worried about going home to see my parents, he said, "Just go there and do exactly what they do. If they sit in front of the TV all day, sit next to them and watch TV. Make the visit as short as you need to, but relax with the situation and join in fully."

That was Rinpoche's general advice: Don't separate yourself. He wasn't saying we should buy into everyone's views and opinions, but he saw disdaining other people and the way they live as an unnecessary type of ego reinforcement.

His advice enhanced my relationship with my parents, and over the years I've given it to many people. When there's a struggle, the parents hate it as much as the children. But if you join in, they feel that you're not rejecting their lifestyle. They feel appreciated. You don't have to talk about politics or religion. You don't have to complain because they're not interested in your life. You just join in with their routine.

The poet Allen Ginsberg was a close student of Rinpoche's. Near Boulder, Colorado, where he lived, there was a big manufacturing complex for making nuclear weapons called Rocky Flats. He would go there to protest by sitting on the railroad tracks. When Rinpoche talked about "joining in" during public teachings, Allen would raise his hand and Rinpoche would call on him. They'd have a conversation about the pros and cons of joining in, and Rinpoche would say, "Allen, if you want to effect change, you should get a job at Rocky Flats."

Sometimes Rinpoche used the word *infiltrate*, which maybe gets a little more at what he was communicating to Allen. If you really want something to change, join in and connect with people's minds and hearts. Find out who it is that you're having a problem with. To reject or set yourself apart inevitably comes with a kind of arrogance or disdain, what Rinpoche calls **attitudinal problems**. "We're doing it right, and you're doing it wrong. We're the together ones, and you're the ones causing all the problems."

This is a challenging idea. Suppose you're protesting against something that is clearly harmful to people or animals or the environment. Rinpoche would still say to infiltrate, join in, know the people. We're all in this together, and in order to be able to communicate in a skillful way, a way that might allow for change, we have to see the situation from all sides.

The documentary *Control Room*, about Al Jazeera and the war in Iraq, features an American soldier who has a breakthrough in understanding his own bias. The American public was understandably outraged to see bodies of dead American soldiers on the news, and this soldier felt the same way. Then he realized that seeing the images of dead Iraqi civilians didn't have the same impact on him because he didn't see Iraqis as "his" people. This realization shook him. He understood then that nothing would ever change unless we started considering things from each other's point of view, unless we tried to go beyond the setup of "us and them."

Following this discussion of the two unhelpful attitudes around work, Rinpoche talks about work as part of our spiritual practice. Work, he says, can become **a source of inspiration**. The instruction he gives mirrors his instructions on mindfulness and awareness. The mindfulness aspect concerns precision, which he expresses here as **feeling the earth**. The awareness aspect concerns once again connecting with space.

This is how Rinpoche says we should live our life: being right on the dot, fully present, but at the same time, having a sense of the whole environment. He says, **If you do not feel that every step, every situation reflects your state of mind, and therefore has spiritual significance, then the pattern of your life becomes full of problems.**

Connecting with the earth means connecting precisely with all the details of your life. As an example, he uses the Japanese tea ceremony, which involves precise mindfulness in making, offering, and drinking tea. The tea ceremony is like an art form, but it can be used as a model for everyday life—that kind of presence and appreciation of all the details of your life.

Let's say you're in the office, and it's just another day, and you're completely caught up in your mind. This is a common experience, but now you practice coming back to being fully present, right where you are: with your fingers on the keyboard, with the sound of the phone ringing, with the expression on your coworker's face, with the door opening and shutting. You come back to the quality of the light, the smells, the feeling of the room, its colors and shapes. You just keep bringing yourself back to being fully present to the details and to the total environment.

I find this an extremely useful practice. Whatever is happening in my life, there are always sounds to be heard, sights to be seen, textures to be felt, and there is always the space in which all those occur. I can be there for all of it. Instead of being caught up in my mental chatter, I can touch the earth and feel the space simultaneously. This is the basic instruction for connecting with the openness of a continual meditative state.

Then Rinpoche makes an important point, which is that **the way to practice is not to concentrate upon things nor**

to try to be aware of yourself and the job at the same time. He's not advising being self-conscious about the details of your life—such as being rigid about how your fingers hit the keyboard: "Don't bother me, I'm being mindful." You can get so stressed out being mindful that you say, "This is impossible! How can I be mindful when the door is opening fifteen times per minute?" So Rinpoche again makes the point that mindfulness has to be combined with awareness: **Awareness in work is very important**, he says. **This depends very much upon feeling the earth and the space together.**

When you begin to acknowledge this combination of precision and openness while you're working, **you begin to feel that there is more room in which to do things.** Interestingly enough, when you practice in this way, you also begin to feel that there is more time. So much of our claustrophobia, franticness, panic, and stress is mentally created. Of course, our lives are packed, but it's the mind component that's really driving us crazy. Working with our mind changes our perception of reality. A fearful mind perceives a threatening world; an angry mind perceives a hostile, provocative world; a relaxed mind sees life as far more workable.

Rinpoche then goes on to elaborate further on connecting with openness as you are working. **You don't have to try to hold on to it or try to bring it about deliberately, but just acknowledge that vast energy of openness with a fraction-of-a-second flash to it.** That "fraction-of-a-second flash" is an interesting practice instruction. At the time, I don't think most of his audience knew what it meant—I certainly didn't. But it stuck in my mind and intrigued me.

First, you become more familiar with the meditative state of mind through your sitting practice. Then you begin to realize that you can tune in to that state at any time. You don't concentrate until you get this special "timeless" feeling. You tune in for a fraction-of-a-second flash and then relax. You tune in and relax, over and over again. Then, as Rinpoche says so beautifully in *Shambhala: The Sacred Path of the Warrior*, "If you are able to relax—relax to a cloud by looking at it, relax to a drop of rain and experience its genuineness—you can see the unconditionality of reality, which remains very simply in things as they are, very simply."

Rinpoche makes the point that when we have this kind of open awareness, we should not split ourselves in two, between the watcher and the doer. We should be "one with": one with the open sky, one with whatever we are doing. As you can see, this "one with" instruction comes up repeatedly.

We can always slow down and have "appreciative perception," as Rinpoche said in *Shambhala: The Sacred Path of the Warrior*. We can appreciate the light falling on the table, the smell of fallen leaves in autumn, the raucous voice of the crow, the lengthening shadows in the late afternoon. There is a kind of atmosphere that you can feel when you have awareness of the details and the vast space in which they occur.

LOVE

IN THE ORIGINAL talk that became this section, Rinpoche said, "The primal ground is filled with powerful energy, a reserve of unconditioned warmth when not manipulated by ego." In *The Myth of Freedom*, this has been edited to say, **There is a vast store of energy which is not centered, which is not ego's energy at all.**

There is a vast store of energy, a reserve of unconditioned warmth, that doesn't belong to anyone and doesn't have to be fixated on *me* and *you*. **This energy**, he says, **is always ongoing.** Whether or not you're aware of it, and **whether or not it is seen through the confused filter of ego**, it's always available.

The preceding chapter was mostly about working with the energy of negativity. This section is about the energy of love, intimacy, passion. It's about the energy of connection. To work with this requires not grasping to the energy in a dualistic way—which Rinpoche calls **captive energy**—but allowing it to flow freely. For example, in a relationship, captive energy would be getting too invested in how you want things to evolve. On the other hand, letting the energy flow freely would manifest as a wait-and-see attitude, a curiosity about what will happen next.

When this powerful energy becomes fixated and solidified, it turns into **neurotic passion**. When it becomes all about *me* wanting to seduce *you*, then real communication can't happen. It's no longer about love or intimacy or heartfelt communication. It's about you getting what you want and not considering the other person's feelings at all.

But, Rinpoche says, if you let the energy flow, it is experienced as "free passion" (not to be confused with the "free love" that was popular in those days). The following analogy has always stuck in my mind:

Free passion is radiation without a radiator, a fluid, pervasive warmth that flows effortlessly. . . . By opening, by dropping our self-conscious grasping, we see not only the surface of an object, but we see the whole way through. He talks about this here as genuine, true communication and expands on this theme in the next section, "Working with People."

With **whole-way-through communication**, you really see a person, not just the surface, not just based on sexual attraction or whether you like the way they look—not like online dating and all the agony that puts people through. Instead, you appreciate the qualities of the other person, their personality, their timidity or bluntness, their ruggedness or sophistication.

But, Rinpoche warns, sometimes the other person won't like this. They may find it threatening to have you see them all the way through. Then he says an interesting thing: **If that person runs away from you, that is their way of communicating with you.**

The likely cause of the problem, he says, is that you don't have a sense of humor: **What is wrong is that you do not see all sides of the situation and therefore miss the humorous and ironical aspect.** Your humorless whole-way-through communication may come across as intimidating to the other person, causing them to run away. If you chase after them, they'll see you as grasping, needy, aggressive, and they'll run even farther. Instead, allow the other person to communicate with you in their own style. Wait and see what happens when you slow down and let them be.

Sense of humor is a big topic for Rinpoche. There's a whole chapter on it in *Cutting Through Spiritual Materialism*. It's basically a sign of an open, flexible mind that you can see the funny side, for instance, of somebody being so scared of you that they take off running. When you can see yourself as they see you, maybe you'll cringe, but maybe you'll also have a good laugh.

The approach Rinpoche suggests is to **dance with reality, dance with apparent phenomena**. You allow the dance to unfold as it unfolds. You loosen your grip, let go of control, and allow the dance to unfold.

When you're with another person, **instead of impulsively making a move from your side, you allow a move from the other side, which is learning to dance with the situation. You do not have to create the whole situation; you just watch it, work with it, and learn to dance with it.**

Making a sudden, impulsive move usually comes from fear—fear that you're going to lose something, that the relationship isn't going your way. If there is neediness or aggression, then true love, intimacy, and communication begin to break down—not just between sexual partners but also between parents and children or between friends.

Once Dzigar Kongtrul Rinpoche gave a talk about the teacher-student relationship where he said, "I think all the students are either suckers or skippers." Suckers are needy—

you want, you want, you want from the teacher. Skippers don't want to get close. (I am more this type.) You say, "Will you be my teacher?" but you're always making sure that you're not close enough for them to give you advice you don't want to hear. When either of these scenarios are functioning, what results is a very awkward, very clumsy dance.

The advice Rinpoche gives in this section is the best relationship guide you could hope for. Try it. Try dancing rather than controlling, and you'll see.

WORKING WITH PEOPLE

THIS SECTION IS about how to benefit other people. The precision and openness he talks about in "Work" and what he says about dancing in "Love" apply to a wide variety of life situations, including being of genuine benefit to others.

All of this requires maturity. It requires loving-kindness toward ourselves, trust in ourselves. Here, Rinpoche says that poor communication is a result of feeling bad about ourselves. I think that's one to write in your notebook. When we feel bad about ourselves, we feel we need to put barbed wire around our territory for protection. Either that or **we march straight through into another person's territory, disregarding the proper conditions for entering it. There might be signs saying, "Keep off the grass, no trespassing." But each time we see these signs, they make us more aggressive, more revolutionary.**

Instead of following this futile approach, Rinpoche gives a process of three stages leading to what he calls "selfless help." This means being able to work selflessly for others rather than follow our own agenda for how we want them to be. Any of us trying to help people who need help know what a trap it is to want things to work out according to our agenda. They keep relapsing, or being angry, or not changing in the way we want them to, so we burn out because they're not fulfilling our dream.

Once I was the meditation instructor for a sweet young man named Michael. He had lost one eye, seriously injured his back twice, and had broken many of his bones. He was in constant pain and had become addicted to his medication. I thought my job was to save him. When he kept relapsing, I mentioned my disappointment to Rinpoche. It was the only time he ever got angry with me. He became extremely stern and said loudly, "Don't ever have expectations for other people!" Then he softened a bit and said, "Just be kind to Michael. Invite him for tea. Try to make his life a little easier."

Rinpoche's three-part process, which also applies to communication in a love relationship, is a very compassionate approach. Its first step is cultivating maitri, extending warmth toward ourselves, what His Holiness the Dalai Lama describes as "self-compassion."

For Rinpoche, maitri meant accepting yourself just as you are, not rejecting any part of yourself. This friendship with yourself is so unconditional that it becomes the basis for unconditional friendship with other people. If you accept yourself completely, then you can accept others completely. This is the first step, but it's also a lifetime's work. For a long time, I used to teach nothing but maitri, but then I thought it was time to move on. Now I'm not so sure.

The second step is genuine communication. When you know yourself so well that you've seen it all, then you no longer have to protect yourself. When you don't put up barriers, it becomes possible to stand in another person's shoes. You can communicate openly because even if they trigger you, that won't set off a chain reaction and send you into a tailspin. We all get triggered, but we can see this simply as *shenpa* arising, as attachment arising. It doesn't have to go any further—into "bad," "good," "should," or "shouldn't."

Having maitri and genuine communication as a basis, you can help others without your agenda getting in the way. In this **third stage of selfless help, true compassion, we do not do things because it gives us pleasure but because things need to be done. . . . It is not for them or for me. It is environmental generosity.**

If we have maitri as a base, when the neurotic pattern arises, our intelligence and wisdom become stronger than our emotional reactivity. Generally speaking, our emotional reactivity clouds our intelligence and wisdom. Our intelligence just goes underground, and we blindly do the thing that will make ourselves and others suffer. These teachings give us an alternative.

At the end of "Working with People," Rinpoche summarizes the teaching in two sentences: **If we can make friends with ourselves, if we are willing to be what we are, without hating parts of ourselves and trying to hide them, then we can begin to open to others. And if we can begin to open without always having to protect ourselves, then perhaps we can begin to really help others.**

THE EIGHTFOLD PATH

THE EIGHTFOLD PATH is a set of practices from the Buddha's first teaching after attaining enlightenment, his statement of the Four Noble Truths. It is an explanation of the fourth noble truth: "the truth of the path leading to the cessation of suffering." I came across the eightfold path for the first time in Rinpoche's *Garuda* magazine in an article that later turned into this section of *The Myth of Freedom*.

I didn't realize how unconventional Rinpoche's presentation was until sometime later, when I was studying Buddhist teachings with a college professor. He asked each of us to give a talk, so I cheerfully volunteered to do the teaching on the eightfold path because I had been so inspired by the *Garuda* article. But when I gave the talk, the professor couldn't understand what in the world I was talking about. The only thing that he seemed to recognize were the names of the eight.

When he spoke about the Buddhist path, Rinpoche would sometimes make the point that this path is not "ready-made." As he says in the *Profound Treasury of the Ocean of Dharma*, "The nature of the path is more like an expedition or exploration than following a road that already has been built." The path just develops organically as we go along. The "journey," he says in *Shambhala: The Sacred Path of the Warrior*, is "like a flower unfolding   it is a natural process of expansion."

The eight aspects of the path are right view, right intention, right speech, right discipline, right livelihood, right effort, right mindfulness, and right samadhi. Rinpoche emphasizes that **we first must understand what Buddha meant by "right." He did not mean to say right as opposed to wrong at all. He said "right" meaning "what is," being right without a concept of what is right.**

"Right" here means things just as they are. It's like the meaning of "basic goodness" in the Shambhala teachings. Basic goodness is basic because it transcends the biases of both good and bad. Similarly, in the eightfold path, "right" transcends right and wrong. This is leading us in the direction of understanding what an unfabricated, unbiased, inconceivable state of mind would feel like, what that would be experientially.

In the first chapter of *The Myth of Freedom*, the cause of suffering is presented as running away from life as it is. In particular, it is running away from insecurity, groundlessness, discomfort, and unpredictability—trying to avoid them and pretend that they're not there, that they don't pervade our lives. Trying to avoid the unavoidable brings suffering. The eightfold path is the path to the cessation of suffering, the path to the cessation of struggle and avoidance. It is the path that allows us to embrace life as it is.

Rinpoche begins "The Eightfold Path" with one of his recurring themes, the theme of no exits. Usually we don't want to stay on the path. We don't want to be just where we are. We're always looking for an alternative.

He makes a humorous analogy about being on a highway: **The signs say: "Tibetan Village, next exit"; "Japanese Village, next exit"; "Nirvana, next exit"; "Enlightenment,**

next exit—instant one"; "Disneyland, next exit." If you turn right, everything is going to be okay. You get what you are promised. But after having gone to Disneyland or having taken part in the Nirvana Festival, then you have to think about how you are going to get back to your car, how you are going to get home. You have to get back on the highway and relate again to life as it is.

Some of us enter into our spiritual traditions hoping to avoid being who we are and where we are. But, as Rinpoche says, **Buddhism promises nothing. It teaches us to be what we are where we are, constantly, and it teaches us to relate to our living situations accordingly.** It may take many years before we hit the wall of realizing that we have to get back on the highway and relate to life as it is. Our Buddhist practice—whether it's vipashyana, Zen, or a Tibetan practice—was never meant to be an escape from being who and where we are. But for many of us, that lesson is a long time coming.

RIGHT VIEW

The first aspect of the eightfold path is *right view*. In his book *The Heart of the Buddha's Teaching*, which presents these eight aspects more traditionally, Thich Nhat Hanh says, "Right View is, first of all, a deep understanding of the Four Noble Truths—our suffering, the making of our suffering, the fact that our suffering can be transformed, and the path of transformation."

In *The Myth of Freedom*, Rinpoche explains right view in terms of having a direct relationship with reality, free of our opinions and interpretations. His Holiness the Dalai Lama is a good example of this. He follows current events avidly to stay informed. But, as Dzigar Kongtrul Rinpoche says, when His Holiness watches the news, he simply watches the news. Instead of getting worked up, he sees the news as it is, without letting his personal slant get in the way. That leaves room for understanding what he's witnessing from someone else's perspective.

We will predictably continue to have our views and opinions, and the shenpa—the reactive heat—that comes along with that. We could, however, start to understand that what we're thinking is not the absolute truth but just our opinion, just our personal slant.

As an example of right view, Rinpoche talks about not judging someone walking toward you as good or bad. As he says, **The philosophical attitude could be just to see the situation as it is. "That person walking toward me is not a friend, therefore he is not an enemy either. He is just a person approaching me. I don't have to prejudge him at all." That is what is called "right view."**

If you see the person as an enemy, you have to realize that "enemy" is just your current opinion. They may be coming to attack you, or they may be coming to apologize. Why don't you wait and see? Of course, you have to be intelligent and realistic about what's going on. If someone is coming at you with a knife, you act appropriately. But that doesn't mean justifying a closed heart.

Rinpoche is talking about keeping a fresh state of mind. This is the same state of mind that Thich Nhat Hanh refers to in his book when he says, "From the viewpoint of ultimate reality, Right View is the absence of all views."

RIGHT INTENTION

The second aspect of the eightfold path is *right intention*. The Buddhist teachings stress the importance of the intention behind our actions. Rinpoche describes intention as **a thought process which relates thinking to acting. When you encounter a situation, you think; and thinking inclines toward acting.**

In our example, wrong intention would be based on the view that the person walking toward you is either a friend or an enemy. **Having conceptually fixed the person,** Rinpoche says, **now you are ready either to grasp or attack him. Automatically there is an apparatus functioning to provide either a waterbed or a shotgun for that person.**

Right intention means not being inclined toward anything other than exactly what is occurring in the moment, neither more nor less. It is the openness of mind and heart to let people be who they are, knowing that we are all in process. As Katharine Hepburn once said, "The time to make up your mind about people is never."

Thich Nhat Hanh makes the same connection between right view and right intention (which he calls "right thinking"). "Right Thinking," he says, "is thinking that is in accord with Right View. It is a map that can help us find our way."

RIGHT SPEECH

The third aspect is *right speech*. The classical explanation of right speech, according to Thich Nhat Hanh, has four parts:

speaking truthfully, not speaking with a "forked tongue" (not saying one thing to one person and something else to another), not speaking cruelly, and not exaggerating or embellishing.

In *The Myth of Freedom*, Rinpoche doesn't say anything about the content of right speech. Instead, his emphasis is on keeping your communication clear and simple. You say "yes" or "no," not "maybe." You don't fill up the space with your words. You don't fill it up with your neuroses. Right speech

implies perfect communication, communication which says, "It is so," rather than, "I think it is so." "Fire is hot," rather than, "I think fire is hot." Fire *is* hot, automatically—the direct approach. . . . Nobody would have to say, "I think it is dark outside" or "You must believe it is dark outside." You would just say, "It is dark outside."

It can be quite revealing to notice how much you try to protect yourself by how you communicate. When I served as the first director of Gampo Abbey, I drove people crazy with my indirect, manipulative way of communicating what I needed done. Instead of being straightforward, I would say things like, "Do you happen to be going to the workshop? I wouldn't want to take you out of your way, but if you have the time, I'd appreciate getting the tall ladder."

One day, someone said to me, "Cut it! Just cut it, Ani Pema. Cut all your people-pleasing talk. What is it you want me to do? Just tell me!" It was shocking and painful, but I sure got the message. I immediately saw my tendency to manipulate people with my sweetheart style instead of asking directly for what I wanted so they could say, "Yes, I can" or "No, I can't."

RIGHT DISCIPLINE

The fourth aspect is *right discipline*, which Thich Nhat Hanh calls "right action," describing it as "the practice of touching love and preventing harm, the practice of nonviolence toward ourselves and others."

Rinpoche points out that discipline is usually about trying to improve ourselves. Some of us are willing to be disciplined and give up a lot if we think it will result in our being able to leave everything we don't like behind. Right discipline, on the other hand, is more like letting go and opening. It means becoming free of bias and opinion about who we are and who other people are. We practice allowing ourselves to be without our internal dialogue about being "bad," about always "messing up," about "getting it right this time." We also allow other people to be who they are without similar storylines.

Earlier, I described spending time with my mother in terms of discovering cool boredom. Once I committed to just staying in the room with her, the space opened up. But the other thing that happened was that I became curious about her, about who she was beyond my storylines. She had always been this facade figure whom I had trouble with. That negative attitude had diminished my appreciation for the very kind things she had done for me throughout my life. It had also prevented me from being curious.

How deeply the relationship changed when I started asking her about her life. It turned out she loved to talk about the joys and sorrows of her childhood, about her relationship with her own mother, about how she met my father, and so forth. Now I wish I had recorded it for my grandchildren.

RIGHT LIVELIHOOD

The fifth aspect is *right livelihood.* This is generally about not working in a profession that brings harm to living beings or to the earth. Thich Nhat Hanh says, "To practice Right Livelihood, you have to find a way to earn your living without transgressing your ideals of love and compassion."

When Rinpoche talks about right livelihood, however, he emphasizes once again joining in and not setting yourself apart. **People who reject the materialism of American society and set themselves apart from it are unwilling to face themselves . . . unwilling to work with the world as it is.** Right livelihood, in this teaching, is just that: being willing to work with the world as it is. This is similar to the advice he gave me about "joining in" when I visited my mother and what he said to Allen Ginsberg about infiltrating the nuclear weapons plant. It comes down to taking an interest in humanity rather than having preconceived ideas. It comes down to reducing polarization and prejudice in the world rather than adding more.

RIGHT EFFORT

Right effort is number six. Thich Nhat Hanh says this is "the kind of energy that helps us realize the Noble Eightfold Path." As Rinpoche defines it, right effort means fully participating with delight. This is similar to the paramita of exertion, which is also translated as "joyful effort" or "enthusiasm." (The paramitas are the main activities of those on the mahayana path. I will talk about them at length in the next chapter.) Right effort **is seeing a situation precisely as it is at that very moment, being present fully, with delight, with**

a grin. Even though there is effort involved—in meditation, for instance—it's a balanced, uplifted effort.

Generally, when we sit down to meditate, we have a sense of the continuous flow of discursive thoughts. With practice, we begin to realize that there are gaps in the flow. You're completely lost in thoughts, and then, making no effort of your own, your mind naturally comes back. You realize that gaps in the discursiveness happen naturally. You don't make them happen. You touch the breath and let it go. You stay present, and when you wander off, at some point there's a gap, and you find that you've come back, effortlessly.

You notice that there are natural gaps and also that you can create a gap by pausing and having a moment free of being caught up. Rinpoche talks about this as **effort, non-effort and effort, non-effort**. You don't fall into either extreme of trying too hard or not trying hard enough. It's similar to the meditation instruction, "not too tight, not too loose." The effort doesn't become too effortful; the non-effort doesn't become too laid back, where you never do anything. If it's only effort, there's too much "my" project. But only non-effort is also too much about *me*, about my not wanting to be bothered.

In another talk that he gave around the same time, Rinpoche said, "With right effort, if you're in the river and you're being swept along, you can't just float. You have to swim." You don't struggle against the flow of the river, but you also don't just float. You let the river carry you, and at the same time, you swim toward shore. In meditation, gaps naturally appear, but then you have to make an effort to stay present and an effort to come back when you find yourself again lost in discursiveness. Touch the breath, let it go; touch the thoughts, let them go. It's all the play of effort and non-effort.

Rinpoche describes how, as meditators, we're continually seduced by fantasies. **It's all very well to meditate, but how about going to the movies? Meditation is nice, but how about getting together with our friends? How about that?** He says that what's needed here is a gap. What's needed is the space to come up for air and see how we've been swept away.

He then speaks enthusiastically about remedying our discursiveness with right effort: **We are constantly dreaming of infinite possibilities for all kinds of entertainment. There is no room to stop, no room to start providing space. Providing space: effort, non-effort and effort, non-effort—it's very choppy in a sense, very precise, knowing how to release the discursive or visionary gossip. Right effort—it's beautiful.** This instruction is like finger painting, and I find it both evocative and useful.

RIGHT MINDFULNESS

The seventh aspect is *right mindfulness*, which Rinpoche describes more like mindfulness-awareness together. There's space in right effort: opening and relaxing, opening and relaxing, effort and non-effort. But in right mindfulness, there's even more space. **If you are drinking a cup of tea**, he says, **you are aware of the whole environment as well as the cup of tea.** You're fully present and aware of the space all around you. Right mindfulness allows you to relax. As he says poetically, **You have room to dance in the space.** He associates right mindfulness with the creative process—a relaxed, egoless process. Thich Nhat Hanh emphasizes the importance of right mindfulness. When it is present, he says, "the Four Noble Truths and the seven other elements of the Eightfold Path are also present."

RIGHT SAMADHI

Finally, there is *right samadhi*, or "right absorption." Thich Nhat Hanh says that this practice is "to cultivate a mind that is one-pointed." Rinpoche describes right samadhi as **being completely involved, thoroughly and fully, in a nondualistic way. In sitting meditation, the technique and you are one; in life situations, the phenomenal world is also part of you. Therefore, you do not have to meditate as such, as though you were a person distinct from the act of meditating.**

This is related to an instruction he often gave: "Be one with the breath." Let the breath go out into space. Don't concentrate on *you* watching the breath, but feel the breath expanding out. Then feel the next breath going out—touching it and letting it go rather than observing it. This is subtly but profoundly different from meditating **as though you were a person distinct from the act of meditating**. Instead, **if you are one with the living situation as it is, your meditation just automatically happens.**

This "Meditation in Action" chapter has many intriguing instructions. I've been studying these teachings for years and I've never gotten to the bottom of them. If you're feeling the same way, no surprise. And if you think you have gotten to the bottom of them, then try to live by them. You'll find them very useable, though not very graspable.

Q&A

Q: I'm new to the study of Buddhism, so I have this constant nagging sense that not interfering, not acting in any situation where you're invested in how it turns out, seems like not caring how it turns out.

PEMA: That's a good question, and in some way it's accurate. It doesn't really mean not caring in the usual sense, but in the sense of stress, in the sense of falling apart when things don't work out, you definitely aren't so invested. You don't get so worked up about the outcome.

I often think of Rinpoche's advice to "lead your life as an experiment." I love this because it implies that you have an appetite for life because you're very curious about how things will turn out. This approach doesn't have all the negative side effects of wanting things to go a certain way, which is futile and out of your control anyway. We think we have control, but then we're very disappointed when we do everything right and it still doesn't turn out. Instead of going through all that hope and fear, we can be adventurous and wait and see. The natural choreography of life is a lot more interesting and creative than anything we might personally devise.

Q (CONT'D): Then are you trying to preclude disappointment?

PEMA: Not at all. Remember that whole section on the value of disappointment? (See page 21.) The point is to let your present views and opinions, your present investment in the outcome, be challenged a little bit. It's not asking that you adopt new views such as "I shouldn't act in a situation" or "It's wrong to be invested in outcomes," or "I should try to preclude disappointment," but rather you see if you can start going beyond views and opinions altogether.

SIX

THE OPEN WAY

THE BODHISATTVA VOW

WITH THIS CHAPTER, Rinpoche begins to focus on the mahayana path, which he referred to in the first chapter as **the open highway of compassionate action**. As I said earlier, like most Tibetan teachers, Rinpoche taught the three yanas—hinayana (the foundation vehicle), mahayana (the vehicle of compassion and openness), and vajrayana (the fruitional vehicle)—in progressive stages.

A common analogy is building a stone wall: First you need a stable foundation, and then you can carefully pile up stone after stone. In the same way, we start by looking at our pain and how we got stuck in the first place. Building on that, we move on to compassionate action and benefiting others. This was Rinpoche's teaching method, though at the same time, as I've mentioned before, there are certain themes in his presentation that run throughout, no matter what yana he's discussing.

"The Open Way" covers two main topics: the bodhisattva vow, which includes a description of the refuge vow, and the ten *bhumis*. A bodhisattva is a person whose highest aspiration in life is to wake up in order to alleviate the suffering of others and who devotes themselves to compassionate action. The bhumis are ten stages that a bodhisattva goes through, an unfolding process that leads toward complete liberation from neurotic patterns and complete relaxation into the basic ground, that which is unconditional and infinite.

The chapter begins: **Before we commit ourselves to walking the bodhisattva path, we must first walk the hinayana or narrow path.** The hinayana is not "narrow" in the sense of being narrow-minded but in the sense of having no sidetracks. It's like a narrow passage through the mountains, where you can't go right or left because there are massive stone walls on either side that go up as far as you can see. Because there is no wiggle room, you stay present on the dot. The hinayana presents a very pared-down approach. You're either off the track or on the track, either awake or asleep. There's very little gray area. Because of this clarity, you begin to see yourself honestly, with unconditional acceptance. This total acceptance is the key to progressing on the spiritual path.

This path, Rinpoche says, **begins formally with the student taking refuge in the buddha, the dharma, and the sangha—that is, in the lineage of teachers, the teachings, and the community of fellow pilgrims.** In other words, **we expose our neurosis to our teacher, accept the teachings as the path, and humbly share our confusion with our fellow sentient beings.**

The way Rinpoche taught, students would practice sitting meditation for a long time. Ideally they would do a dathün, a monthlong meditation retreat. He also encouraged people after that to do ten-day solo retreats. This intensive practice is something I continue to recommend. When he felt students had come to know themselves well enough through sitting meditation, they could then take the refuge vow if they wished.

Taking the refuge vow is a big step. For some people it happens quickly. That's how it was for me. I'd only been studying the Buddhist teachings for six months when I took the vow with Lama Chimé Rinpoche in England. But others may take years to decide to take the vow. Taking refuge means becoming a Buddhist, which may be exactly what you *don't* want to do. Some people don't want to become anything or join anything, so making this commitment can be quite a stretch.

When we take refuge, Rinpoche says, **symbolically, we leave our homeland, our property and our friends. We give up the familiar ground that supports our ego, admit the helplessness of ego to control its world and secure itself.** He calls this **becoming a refugee**, likening it to leaving home and becoming homeless—not literally leaving our current living situation, our family and friends, but leaving the familiar territory of ego and stepping out into who knows what. When he would give a talk before the refuge vow ceremony, he would often emphasize taking refuge in groundlessness.

I sometimes think that getting used to the feeling of groundlessness is the most significant thing we can do on the spiritual path. Instead of running away from that threatening feeling of having nothing to hold on to, if we could relax with it and embrace it—if we could say to ourselves, "This is just what I'm feeling, and it's not a problem"—then what different lives we would have.

When we take refuge, instead of joining a Buddhist club, we become **a refugee, a lonely person who must depend upon himself or herself.** As a foundation for our path, Rinpoche writes, **we must make a relationship with loneliness until it becomes aloneness.** Over the years, I have found this distinction between loneliness and aloneness very helpful.

"Loneliness" points to an uneasy, uncomfortable feeling that we want to get away from—a place where emotionally we don't want to be. But instead of looking for something to fill up the emptiness of the lonely feeling, we can make a relationship, a friendship, with it. When we become comfortable with the uncertainty inherent in loneliness and no longer feel the urge to get away from it, that is what Rinpoche refers to as "aloneness." (He revisits this topic more fully in the "Tantra" chapter on page 213.)

The next topics are the mahayana and the bodhisattva path. Rinpoche begins by drawing a distinction between the foundation yana and the mahayana: **In the hinayana, the emphasis is on acknowledging our confusion. In the mahayana we acknowledge that we are a buddha, an awakened one, and act accordingly, even though all kinds of doubts and problems might arise.** Acknowledging that we're a buddha is often spoken of as acknowledging our buddha nature; acknowledging, as he says in *Shambhala: The Sacred Path of the Warrior*, that "there is something basically good about our existence as human beings."

In the mahayana, the main attributes or qualities are warmth and openness: the warmth of loving-kindness and compassion and the open-mindedness of shunyata. When we get into the bhumis, the bodhisattva levels, we move deeper and deeper into the experience of shunyata, the natural openness of our being. *Shunyata* is often translated as "emptiness"—not empty like a void but empty of our concepts and beliefs, empty in the sense that nothing can be pinned down as being "like this" or "like that."

Rinpoche goes on to discuss the traditional image of the sun and the clouds. He says, **The basic idea is that, if we are**

going to relate with the sun, which is always shining, **we must also relate with the clouds that**, from our perspective, seem to **obscure the sun. So the bodhisattva relates positively to both the naked sun and the clouds hiding it.** This is an important idea: Both the awake quality and the confusion are equally honored, equally valued.

Up to this point, the teachings in *The Myth of Freedom* have been primarily about the clouds. As he says, **When we try to disentangle ourselves, the first thing we experience is entanglement.** At first, the clouds of confusion feel more prominent than the sun and the sky. However, he's been presenting this not as a problem but as our fundamental working basis, our richness. The confusion is not an obstacle to eradicate but something to know intimately, something to relate to positively.

To relate positively, of course, doesn't mean acting out because of the confusion. But you don't repress anything either. Instead, you find what it feels like to rest in the middle, between those two extremes. And guess what? It feels groundless, uncertain, unpredictable. Once Rinpoche wrote a poem that said, "Why can't we proclaim that which is neither false nor true?" That's the idea. Why can't we rest at ease in the space that is free of fixed mind, free of concretizing, free of coming to solid conclusions?

After the refuge vow, the next big step on the path is taking the bodhisattva vow. Rinpoche calls the bodhisattva vow **the starting point in becoming awake**. When we take this vow, we aspire to emulate the bodhisattvas by making the benefit of others our top priority. The fact that, for the mature bodhisattva, this is selfless help, freely given and without expecting thanks, makes it a big leap for most of us. Therefore, in the beginning we're more like "bodhisattvas-in-training." We know we'll make mistakes, but we're willing to learn and we don't give up when we confront failure. That is the ideal.

To be honest, many people, including myself, have taken the vow naively. We sincerely want to lessen the suffering of others, but we have no idea how challenging that's going to be. Are we really ready to go out on a limb for another person, especially if we're feeling tired and cranky? Are we really willing to give up our privacy? The student starts with some ideal about helping and has to relax with the fact that it can take a long time for that ideal to be realized.

In the next section, Rinpoche says that **sometimes . . . beginning bodhisattvas have second thoughts about such a daring decision** to take a vow to save all sentient beings from the pain of samsara. **This hesitation is described metaphorically in the *sutras* as standing in the doorway of your house, having one foot out in the street and the other foot inside the house. That moment is the test of whether you go beyond the hesitation and step out into the no-man's-land of the street or decide to step back into your familiar home ground.**

Shantideva, the eighth-century sage who wrote *The Way of the Bodhisattva*, a text I often teach from, says that hesitating is actually a good idea. One shouldn't take this vow without exploring it thoroughly. But once you're sure that trying to alleviate suffering is a priority, then, he says, you should go for it without waffling. **Then,** as Rinpoche says, **we are ready to leap on to the bodhisattva path, to open to the joy of working with sentient beings including oneself.**

The bodhisattva vow, Rinpoche says, **acknowledges confusion and chaos—aggression, passion, frustration, frivolousness—as part of the path. The path is like a busy,**

broad highway, complete with roadblocks, accidents, construction work, and police. This is the spiritual path he's talking about, but it sounds a lot like your life, doesn't it?

Rinpoche challenges us to keep our door open—both metaphorically and literally. The idea is not to hide away, not to protect ourselves from the demands of others. I once heard him say that he never had any privacy, and he was fine with that.

"From today onward until the attainment of enlightenment I am willing to live with my chaos and confusion as well as with that of all other sentient beings. I am willing to share our mutual confusion." So no one is playing a one-upmanship game. The bodhisattva is a very humble pilgrim who works in the soil of samsara to dig out the jewel embedded in it. Compassionate action is not a matter of the strong helping the weak but a relationship between equals. It's a mutual journey.

HEROISM

THE REST OF THIS chapter is devoted to the ten bhumis, ten deepening levels of awareness that lead to full awakening. In "Heroism," the emphasis is on the joyful first bhumi and the paramita of generosity. But this section also includes teachings on the ten levels of awareness in general.

These teachings are not about a distant, unattainable citadel but rather describe the unfolding journey of a bodhisattva on the path. They describe a journey that begins even at the pre-bodhisattva level, and they are definitely relevant to you and me right now. The bhumis are different steps in the bodhisattva's journey of learning how to relieve suffering. We can see this teaching as an up-close look at the process we'll inevitably go through as our habitual patterns and overwhelming emotions begin to lose their power.

For a long time, I had zero interest in this topic. One reason is because it seems to have this flavor: "The bodhisattvas on the bhumis are always loving and compassionate, so they are never hooked." I would think, "That doesn't sound like me, even under the best conditions. What use is it to hear that? I need to know how I can get there—I, who am not always loving and compassionate and who does get hooked."

I avoided these teachings because they seemed so beyond my reach. I only became interested in this topic when

I listened to a teaching by Dzigar Kongtrul Rinpoche, who presented the progression through the bhumis as a gradual wearing out of the veils obscuring the fundamental openness of our mind and heart. Since that was something I was already trying to do, suddenly the bhumis felt less remote.

I've since realized how beneficial it can be to learn about things like this that seem way beyond us. The point of such teachings is to sow a seed in our unconscious, which will slowly begin to ripen. "Fruitional" teachings—teachings about the elusive endpoint of the path—can stretch us and point us in a positive direction. Since all of us have the potential to awaken, hearing even a little bit about the bodhisattva levels can create the causes and conditions that help us uncover that potential. Knowing that other people, who were initially just as confused as we often are, have experienced awakening can give us confidence in our own ability to do so.

The first bhumi is characterized by a direct experience of shunyata. You perceive the world, yourself, your emotions—everything—vividly. You see everything free of concepts, views, likes and dislikes, opinions, and philosophical paddings. It's direct experience, just as it is, and it's a mind-blower.

In the teachings about the bodhisattva path, shunyata is one of the main topics. My feeling now is that if we never heard about it, we probably wouldn't recognize it when it occurred. Instead, it would frighten us because it would have no context. It would seem to jump out of nowhere, and we wouldn't know what was happening. That groundlessness could be very scary.

Many years ago, I had an experience of shunyata before I had ever heard that word. It came about thanks to some marijuana and a person I will refer to as "Don Juan."

I was alone in a remote house in the country, and I still remember the experience because it was so startling. I thought to myself, "Nothing is confirming me." Everything was just like it had always been, except that something was missing—whatever usually confirmed me and made me feel grounded. I knew I wasn't in control, and I was so scared I walked three miles to my nearest friend's house seeking comfort. Of course this wasn't a stable experience of shunyata; it was more like a glimpse of shunyata, or a "first-bhumi shock."

It's not so uncommon for people to have glimpses of shunyata, either during meditation or when there's a sudden shock like a car accident or a loss that comes out of the blue. Sometimes the glimpse is thrilling, and sometimes it's scary. But a genuine first-bhumi experience is more than that. It means you never fall back. Never again do you see things the way you did before. It's a complete, stabilized, irreversible experience of things as they are. And most importantly it's joyful, very joyful.

When I first heard about the ten bhumis, the first thing that came to my mind was "Why ten?" Having the irreversible realization of things as they are seemed good enough for me. Why did there have to be nine more levels? There are a few ways to answer this question.

The first is that after the breakthrough first-bhumi experience, there is still a subtle dualistic sense of acknowledging your experience, a subtle concept of observing what is happening. Therefore, Rinpoche says, **the bodhisattva must go through ten stages of development to cut through the watcher, the acknowledger**.

The transition from being a bodhisattva-in-training to a bodhisattva on the first bhumi is dramatic, but as we progress further, what happens from each bhumi to the next is very subtle. In his book *Work, Sex, and Money*, Rinpoche says, "The bodhisattvas move from one bhumi to the next by seeing that their previous involvement was a trip and then stepping out of it. Then they get involved in another trip, and they step out of that one as well. And so it goes, on and on."

At each stage, we have a view of how things are, and after a while, inevitably, we become attached to this view. To progress through the bhumis, or on the spiritual path in general, we have to let go over and over again. We have to allow the rug to be pulled out from under us whenever we get fixated on our current way of seeing. As we do so, we gain more and more access to open space, to the openness of our mind. This process can happen in one lifetime or over the course of many.

Another way of looking at the need for ten stages is that it takes time to be able to communicate our realization. When you arrive at the bhumis—so I'm told—your passion to end suffering in the world becomes a powerful motivating force because you see that so much of the suffering is unnecessary. You can see the emptiness of all things and then immediately want to convey your experience. But it takes a long time to develop the ability to speak and act in a way that will actually benefit people. The first-bhumi experience may feel like enlightenment, but it's only a stage along the way. From there, you have to join your wisdom with skillful means so that your words really communicate to the heart.

It's said that when the Buddha attained enlightenment, he described his experience to the first person he met in this way: "I have found a dharma like ambrosia, deep, peaceful, simple, uncompounded, radiant." The person said, "Oh, that's very interesting," and went on his way. It was like, "Well, it doesn't do me any good, but I'm glad you're happy."

Even though the Buddha had attained complete enlightenment, the final stage after the tenth bhumi, he still felt at first that there was no way to communicate what he had discovered. Quite quickly he understood that he needed to begin by teaching about confusion and pain. At that point everybody got interested because that's where they were at: They wanted to know about how to be free of suffering. So his first teaching was on the Four Noble Truths—the truths of suffering, the cause of suffering, the cessation of suffering, and the eightfold path to that cessation.

Each of the bhumis is related to one of the ten paramitas. In Rinpoche's presentation, rather than saying much about the actual bhumi, he teaches mostly about its associated paramita.

The word *paramita* literally means "going to the other shore," going beyond the usual preconceptions that blind us to our immediate experience. They are like a raft that carries us across the river of confusion. Usually there are six paramitas, but sometimes, as in this teaching, that list is expanded to ten. The first six are generosity, discipline, patience, exertion, meditation, and prajna (knowledge). The four additional ones are skillful means, vision, power, and wisdom.

The paramitas are activities in which the bodhisattva trains. They are the tools, you could say, that the bodhisattva uses to alleviate the suffering of others. They describe the compassionate conduct of a bodhisattva and are simultaneously ways of relaxing with the fundamental unpredictability of our lives. In the context of the bhumis, these paramitas describe the main activity that we engage in, the main activity that we use to let go into openness, into shunyata.

On the first bhumi, the main activity is generosity, which is a practice of letting go of holding on to yourself. We give to others not only to benefit them but also to let go of anything we're holding on to. Generosity involves stretching beyond where it's currently comfortable, letting go of the attitude that "I'll give this much, but not more." Of course it's essential to give food, clothing, shelter, and so on to those who don't have them. And it's powerful, at a more fundamental, egoless level, when something in you wants to hold on to just a little for yourself, and instead you stretch. Metaphorically and literally, you open your tightly clenched fist and you give.

In the tradition Rinpoche established, stretching beyond your comfort was included in the bodhisattva vow ceremony. He asked everyone who took the vow to give a gift that was hard to let go of. This was Rinpoche's creative inspiration; it wasn't part of the traditional vow. If you give money, you give more than is comfortable. You can give any prized possession that you don't want to let go of. When I've been a preceptor for this vow, I've received some pretty interesting gifts, including many packs of cigarettes and a few chain saws.

The joyous generosity of the first bhumi, Rinpoche says, **is accompanied by prajna, transcendental knowledge.** When we arrive at the first bodhisattva level, we see things directly as they are—we experience shunyata—and this clear seeing, or prajna, infuses our generosity practice. The paramita of prajna is specifically associated with the sixth bhumi, but it's an integral feature of all ten paramitas. The view of seeing things as they are, without any conceptual overlay, permeates the whole path from the first bhumi until enlightenment.

From this point on, the bodhisattva practices all the paramitas with what is called the threefold purity—no big deal about the doer, no big deal about the action, and no big deal about the result. In terms of generosity, this means first not making a big deal about the giver, not having any ideas of "I am the generous one." This is a common tendency that we can recognize in ourselves: Our giving is often accompanied by the sense that we're being virtuous.

Practicing generosity infused with prajna undercuts the concept of being the generous one. There's also no big deal about the gift and no big deal about how the gift is received. The latter can be hard because you have to let go of being concerned with the response. Instead of getting a thank-you note, you might get "Why did you give me this? What were you thinking?" Or commonly these days, you might get no acknowledgment at all.

The path through the ten bhumis is a path of letting go of all our concepts, including the concept of ourselves as a person progressing through these stages. It's a path of relaxing into a completely open state of mind, a state of utter simplicity. The first big breakthrough in this process happens when we have the first-bhumi experience of shunyata, the stabilized realization that nothing can be pigeonholed, that nothing is fixed, that there is no such thing as a true story.

But the experiences of the bhumis don't just pop up out of nowhere. They happen as a result of the practice you're doing right now. For example, we've been reading teachings on mindfulness, awareness, shamatha, and vipashyana. To the degree that you can put these teachings into practice—letting the breath dissolve into space, touching the thoughts and letting them dissolve, and all the other instructions—to that degree you'll be predisposed to experiencing the expansiveness of the first bhumi.

The word *practice* indicates becoming familiar with open, unbiased mind, becoming familiar with nowness. Instead of practicing daydreaming, we can practice being awake. As Rinpoche says, we can be **fully in the now**.

We do get distracted and our mind does wander, but we have a technique where we keep coming back to the present moment. Rinpoche taught how to be fully present with a sense of the space around our breath, the space around our body, or, in relationships, the space around ourselves and other people. If we practice in this way now, then at some point we'll experience the complete simplicity of shunyata. So, if you read about the bhumis and think, "I'd like to experience that," you can prepare the ground by training in staying present with an open heart and mind.

You may learn, for example, that at a certain stage, the bodhisattva no longer has any shenpa, with its grasping quality. If you'd like to be without shenpa—if you'd like to stop biting the hook and going through all the painful repercussions of that—then you can start by acknowledging when you get hooked right now. You can notice how shenpa comes with a charge and a momentum, and you can practice interrupting that momentum, not some time in the future when you have more time or feel more together but right now.

To start working with our confusion right now, we can begin by becoming more aware of our confusion and acknowledging it. We can come to know our confusion with friendship and self-compassion. We can practice having a light touch and letting go of the struggle.

Everything you're learning, contemplating, or practicing now will point you toward experiencing the bodhisattva levels, the ten bhumis. Wherever you are on the path, do what you're doing fully and completely. Every breath is a breath that could wake you up or put you to sleep. Every thought is the same.

THE SANITY OF EARTH

THE SECOND bodhisattva level, the spotless or stainless bhumi, Rinpoche says, is **based on making friends with oneself, loving oneself**. This is a perfect example of the bhumis not just popping out of nowhere. We are encouraged from the beginning of the path to make friends with ourselves. To be ashamed of ourselves, to not value ourselves, creates so many problems in our lives. At the level of the second bhumi, this warmth, this tenderness and friendship, is fully established. It is no longer something we need to practice. Yet when does that friendship start? It starts right now.

It is said that about halfway through one stage or bhumi, the next stage has already started. In the case of the second bhumi, it seems the shift begins much earlier than that, right from the beginning of our practice. This is because, as Rinpoche says, the purity or spotlessness of the second bhumi is based on loving-kindness to oneself: **You are not a nuisance to yourself anymore; you are good company, an inspiration to yourself.**

The paramita associated with the second bhumi is discipline, again with the threefold purity—no big deal about yourself as the disciplined one, no big deal about the activity of discipline itself, and no big deal about the result of your discipline. It's discipline without ego-clinging, without credentials. **There is no need to try to be pure, to painfully discipline yourself to be pure, to apply detergent to your natural condition. The spotlessness or purity of the second bhumi is realized when you acknowledge your natural purity.**

Rinpoche expands upon the theme of "selfless help," which he introduced earlier in the section called "Working with People." (See page 128.) As I said there, selfless help means helping others without your own agenda getting in the way. Here he says, **The bodhisattva delights in working with people rather than regarding compassionate action as a duty.** There is no dogma about how to act but rather one responds spontaneously to whatever is needed. Most importantly, the bodhisattva's action is never about converting people. The bodhisattva **respects others' lifestyles, speaks their language, and allows them to evolve according to their nature**. It seems to me that this is really good advice wherever you are on your journey.

He follows this by saying something about discipline that I find both humorous and completely true, even for you and me right now: **The bodhisattva will experience strong impulses to tell people how things ought to be.** The discipline, of course, is to not act on those impulses.

Rinpoche again talks about frivolousness, saying something similar to what he said earlier: **Making an additional move is frivolous.** In the context of the second bhumi, however, the lack of impulsiveness is a stabilized state of being. We start where we are right now, holding our seat and feeling the situation we're in completely without acting out of impatience or overexcitement. Gradually this becomes our natural way of being.

As Rinpoche writes, **The test of the bodhisattva's sanity is how directly he or she relates to earth. Anything else is a sidetrack.** In other words, bodhisattvas at this stage know exactly how to relate with their present experience at the kitchen-sink level. Anything less immediate is a spin-off, a way of distracting ourselves. The description here of the second-bhumi bodhisattva gives an inside look at the state of mind and heart of an awake person.

We have the path—our practice and study and our life right now—and we have the fruition of this path. Generally it's best not to look ahead but to be present with what we are doing at this very moment. Then drop by drop, moment by moment, our understanding evolves. Nevertheless, the bhumis are descriptions of the completed form of what we are practicing now. They show us what is possible. Because we all have the potential to awaken, Dzigar Kongtrul Rinpoche says that it's just a matter of time. As he puts it, "Sooner or later, awakening is inevitable."

PATIENCE

THE MAIN PRACTICE of the bodhisattva on the third bhumi is the paramita of patience. As a bodhisattva-in-training, I find it helpful to see what the patience of a bodhisattva—completely uncontrived, natural patience—looks like. It gives me some clues for how I could practice it right on the spot the next time I get provoked.

Rinpoche says that the mature bodhisattva is not in a rush and has the feeling of **having nothing to lose**. There is a sense of waiting to see how the situation progresses when we don't meddle with it. We are not, he says, **being compulsively driven by obligations to keep within time limits**. (Rinpoche himself was quite famous for not being bound by conventional time limits.) If we don't make sudden moves now, if we develop the ability to wait—and, perhaps, even dance with the situation—then there's room for spontaneity and a sense of humor.

Here he tells a story about **the conventional notion of patience**, where you **hold your temper, repressing your restlessness**. When your friends are late for a meeting, you find yourself pacing back and forth, getting more and more worked up and irritated. But when they finally arrive, you act as if there's no problem. **When they say, "I'm sorry I'm late," we say, "Don't mention it. I've been enjoying myself, looking at the scenery, talking to strangers . . ." Although we pretend**

that we are not concerned about the time, actually we are compulsively caught up in living by the clock so our denial of concern and the hiding of our anger is hypocritical.

If this story sounds familiar, we may wonder how we could ever move from this kind of impatience to being able to **just sit patiently without feeling that we are "waiting" for something else to happen**. I've been taught to train with this by connecting with what impatience feels like and developing my capacity to sit still with the restlessness of that energy. This is a really helpful practice. We don't repress our irritation, but we also don't speak or act out of it. We simply become familiar with sitting still with restlessness. Practicing in this way moves us toward egoless patience, genuine patience, where our main concern is being there for others without our emotional responses getting in the way.

The essence of a bodhisattva's patience is captured in Rinpoche's attitude of never giving up on his students. This attitude was why I loved him so much. Seeing him be so patient, even with people who I thought were outrageous, even with people everyone else thought were incorrigible, made me know that he was going to be patient with me too. Patience with whatever people present—that is the third-bhumi patience of the bodhisattva.

In this section, Rinpoche emphasizes that **the ten stages of the bodhisattva's path toward enlightenment should be regarded as landmarks, points of reference on a map, rather than as events to be celebrated, such as birthdays or graduations**. You don't graduate from one to the other and get a medal or certificate to frame and hang on your wall. You can't assess yourself and determine that "now I'm on the third bhumi."

The first bhumi, Rinpoche writes, **is an extremely spectacular experience, a sudden explosion of joy.** But after that, the transition from one bhumi to the next is very hard to pin down. As Rinpoche puts it, **It is a very gentle, very gradual process.** Step by gradual step, our big-sky mind becomes more and more accessible.

TRADITION

IN HIS DESCRIPTION of the fourth bhumi, Rinpoche talks almost entirely about its associated paramita, joyful exertion or enthusiasm—*virya* in Sanskrit. This section returns to a theme Rinpoche brought up in "Work" (see page 119): that we would be wise not to set ourselves apart but rather take interest and delight in working with where we are. I frequently heard him discuss this topic because, as hippies, we tended to be rather dismissive and judgmental about anyone who had not "dropped out" of mainstream conventional society. Rinpoche's message again and again was more like you have to drop in fully in order to drop out intelligently.

As he says, a bodhisattva—and I'd also say a bodhisattva-in-training—does not reject what's happening in society but rather is enthusiastic about getting to know the society and those who make it up. **First,** he says, **we must step into the tradition, must understand it fully, its wise and its foolish aspects, why people are hypnotized by its dogmas; we must understand what wisdom, if any, lies behind the dogma. Then we can step out of it sanely.**

When he'd say these things, I'd always think of how he, a young man born in Tibet and raised in traditional monastic culture until he escaped the country at age twenty, joined so fully and completely into Western traditions and culture. It seemed that he never looked back. He wasn't at all interested in introducing us to Tibetan traditions. His appetite was for finding out how to introduce the essence of the Buddhist teachings into this brand-new culture. He had the enthusiasm—the virya—to see what resonated with his Western students and what didn't, what woke us up and what didn't.

Rinpoche says that bodhisattvas aren't bound by any culture, but at the same time they respect the ethical norms of the society they're in. This is what he chose to stress about the fourth-bhumi bodhisattva experience. **Sanity,** he writes, **lies somewhere between the inhibitions of conventional morality and the looseness of extreme impulse.** Bodhisattvas at this fourth-bhumi level of awareness don't reject or scorn, nor do they side with the status quo. **The bodhisattva takes delight in polarities but doesn't side with any extreme.** Taking delight in our differences without getting captured in any one-sided view—this is something I aspire to. I can start not siding with any extreme views today, or at least give it my best shot.

As Rinpoche writes, **Virya . . . is taking delight in working hard with whatever working base or material we are presented with—our state of mind, our traditions, our society. It is not taking sides for or against our traditions or our state of mind, but it is taking delight in them and working with them.**

ZEN AND PRAJNA

IN THIS SHORT section, Rinpoche covers the fifth, sixth, and seventh bhumis, emphasizing again their accompanying paramitas. He gives the impression that proceeding from one level to the next speeds up at this point—particularly after the seventh bhumi, where a breakthrough happens and many **subtle attitudes** are left behind. In other places I've heard these subtle attitudes described as our attachments, our shenpas, and particularly our attachment to "me" as an ongoing reference point.

The paramita of the fifth bhumi is meditation, but here Rinpoche specifies it as **panoramic awareness**, which is known in Japan as Zen. This is **a state of total involvement without center or fringe**, without separation between self and other, subject and object. Right now, if we're practicing meditation with an object such as breath or sound, we probably have a strong sense of "me" being aware of the object. It's a dualistic, me-you, this-that, subject-object experience. The paramita experience, on the other hand, is **awareness without a watcher**. This is **sane awareness**, he says, as opposed to **neurotic awareness**.

One way we can move our practice in the direction of sane awareness is to follow the instruction I mentioned previously to feel the breath as it goes out into space. Let the breath dissolve into space. Sane awareness comes with a sense of spaciousness, so our meditation can **take place in a very open situation**. This, of course, is the approach to meditation that Rinpoche has been recommending all along.

Anything we can do to move away from binary thinking—such as labeling people and things as good or bad, acceptable or unacceptable—moves us in this open, nondual, simplified direction. Rinpoche describes neurotic awareness as **egocentric watching, knowing what we are doing, knowing where we are supposed to be and how we handle the situation, which is quite a complicated process.**

Sane awareness, on the other hand, **is awareness in the sense that there are very few things to keep track of because everything has been simplified into one situation.** Sane awareness is based on keeping it simple—very, very simple. It is a sense of getting out of our own way and staying present, one with whatever is happening, one with the sights and sounds and smells, one with our bodily sensations and emotions.

Rinpoche's presentation of the sixth bhumi is a discussion of the paramita of prajna—transcendental knowledge, clearly seeing things just as they are, also described as "that which sees shunyata." Prajna has already been mentioned in the context of the earlier paramitas, but at this level, when one reaches the **maturation of prajna**, bodhisattvas gain the clarity to see through **subtle attitudes** reflected in their actions.

Here Rinpoche goes into some detail concerning what he means specifically about these subtle attitudes at the level of the sixth bhumi. Up to this point, he says, bodhisattvas could still be attached to their image—**being extraordinarily compassionate, being smooth and skillful, able to handle any situation . . . being sweet and kind and gentle**. The prajna of the sixth bhumi cuts through all that. It cuts through **any sense of virtue or manipulation, any sense of fixed concepts.**

This reminds me of some advice Rinpoche would frequently give me. Out of nowhere he'd say, "Don't be too religious." Somehow I knew exactly what he meant. As a nun, I could easily try to live up to some ideal of piety, but he continually steered me away from this possibility, encouraging me to take the mahayana view of engaging with the sorrows of the world.

As the cutting-through process of prajna develops, the next stage, the seventh bhumi, also begins to unfold, and with it the paramita of *upaya*, or skillful means, which Rinpoche defines as **the perfect application of method**, the perfect application of our actions, words, and thoughts to benefit others.

Rinpoche warns of the pitfalls that could go along with this deepening of realization if we do not continually self-reflect. Because you have experienced subtler and subtler degrees of shunyata, of moving gradually beyond the sense of this and that, it can possibly become harder to catch yourself when you go astray. When one arrives at the first bhumi, one's emotional upheavals are almost completely left behind. But in this case, Rinpoche is warning us that it's never too late for ego to seduce you. As one moves through the bhumis, the grip of shenpa lessens, but it's not completely gone until the seventh bhumi and beyond, when it lets go entirely. Before this, however, it could still be possible to deceive yourself along the way.

As Rinpoche puts it, **the more perfect you become, the subtler your imperfection**. The more certainty you have in your realization, the less able you might be to see your blind spots, even when others point them out and, most dangerously, even when your own teacher points them out.

I've observed this in some dharma teachers who seemed to me to be close to enlightenment. They were wonderful teachers who came across as being very present, very awake. But they had what I now think of as a tragic flaw, an Achilles heel. There was something in them that they hadn't fully acknowledged, and this blind spot became their downfall. It was almost always because of sex or abuse of power. This was sad to see and also a big lesson for me. I realized that I had to self-reflect courageously and deeply to see all the places where I might be deceiving myself. I also had to be open to feedback. If these wonderful, awake teachers could deceive themselves, then certainly I could do the same.

Rinpoche says that at the seventh bhumi, one fully steps out of spiritual materialism. You'd think that kind of ego gratification would have disappeared in the **explosion of joy** at the first bhumi, but this neurosis is **very slippery and difficult to catch**, and doesn't dissolve completely until the seventh bhumi.

At this point, your realization is finally in sync with your words and actions, and you can finally communicate your understanding to others. This is, in fact, the main activity of the seventh bhumi, the unfolding of skillful means. **Skillful means**, he says, **involves using the cutting through method of prajna as well as developing a sense of the absence of "me" and "that." In other words, there is less sense of journey, less sense of a reference or checking point.**

When bodhisattvas have this level of skillful means, they also have complete confidence, **total confidence without a reference point**, as well as lack of inhibition. **We are not afraid to be.** As we get further and further along in the progressive stages of the ten bhumis, their relevance to our ordinary pre-bhumi life becomes less and less obvious. For me, the most interesting thing at this point is to hear Rinpoche describe what it's like to shed more and more layers of confusion, what it's actually like to become increasingly integrated with our original nature, with the fundamental simplicity that is our home ground.

THE APPROACH TO ENLIGHTENMENT

FINALLY, RINPOCHE describes the paramitas associated with the last bhumis—the eighth, ninth, and tenth. He opens by saying that **the paramita of the eighth bhumi is *monlam***, which means "aspiration" or "vision" in Tibetan. This word refers to **the pregnant aspect of the present, the present possibilities for the future**. There's a sense of limitless possibilities for what might happen at any moment in our lives.

Not only that, but we can also look back at where we've come from. For the bodhisattva, this is very important. Rinpoche stresses that we should never forget where we've come from—what we were like in the past and what we went through to get to this point in our lives. This is what allows us to put ourselves in the shoes of people who are struggling. When we meet people caught in neurotic ups and downs and emotional upheavals, we are able to help them because we know the territory. Having this perspective was part of what gave Rinpoche the ability and the courage never to give up on any of his students.

Rinpoche showed us how a full-fledged bodhisattva manifested compassion, and at the same time, he taught us how we ourselves could be. For the eighth-bhumi bodhisattva, the point of reference is no longer oneself but **the totality of sentient beings.** The bodhisattva, he says, **and all sentient beings are one and the same, so he or she gives up keeping track of who is who, what is what . . . because there is no point in carving out territories.**

While aspiring to experience the interconnected state that he describes here, we can do our best to practice this way today. We can emphasize taking an interest in what's needed and not always being so self-absorbed. There is no point in carving out territories, but when we find ourselves doing exactly that, rather than feeling we've messed up, we can rejoice that we have the honesty to be clear about exactly what we're doing.

The paramita of the ninth bhumi is power, in the sense of **a further expression of the confidence of skillful means.** This is the power that comes when our actions and understanding are in sync, when our deeds and intentions are in harmony. **Skillful means is the confidence to step up to the edge of a cliff, and power is the confidence to leap.** We can take a leap, Rinpoche says, because we are without reference point. We can be daring because we're not checking back to see how we're doing or how we're looking or how other people will judge us.

The experience of a ninth-bhumi bodhisattva is close to enlightenment, but we get glimpses of it all along the way. **Our path becomes an evolutionary process,** Rinpoche writes, **in which further power begins to develop, complete power, enlightened power.** The main point is that this power is infused with compassion. It's the power to enter even the most horrific situations in order to alleviate suffering.

The paramita of the tenth bhumi is wisdom, called *jnana* in Sanskrit and *yeshe* in Tibetan. This is nondual, nonconceptual, timeless awareness. In *Cutting Through Spiritual Materialism*, Rinpoche explains the difference between prajna and jnana: "One cannot regard [jnana] as an external experience. . . . Prajna is knowledge in terms of relativity, and jnana is wisdom beyond any kind of relativity. You are completely one with wisdom; you do not regard it as something educational or something experiential." It is just how you are, and how you live, twenty-four hours a day.

In *The Myth of Freedom*, Rinpoche's brief description of the tenth-bhumi paramita of yeshe ends with the story of a king who foresaw that there would be a powerful storm whose rain would produce madness in all who drank it. The king, therefore, put aside a large supply of clean water, and when the rain fell, everyone went mad except for him. **But after a while,** Rinpoche writes, **he realized that he could not communicate with his subjects because they took the mad world to be real and could smoothly function in the world created by their mutual madness.** (It sounds like the film *The Matrix*.) To the subjects, the king was the crazy one. So he made the decision to drink the water of madness, to join with them completely and not set himself apart as the sane one.

Rinpoche interprets this traditional story as **a rather disappointing way of expressing the realization of enlightenment.** Of the many interpretations I've heard, the one that resonates most deeply with me is as follows. At first, the king protects himself from the rainwater and becomes the sane one watching everyone else go insane. However, the mad subjects live in a consensus reality where all that they're doing seems sane, and it's the king who's acting strangely. The king symbolizes the enlightened being who has to give up the reference point of being the awakened one, the one with the correct point of view, the one not confused and bewildered. The subjects represent all of us poor, suffering beings caught in the mirage of samsara, not even knowing that we're caught.

If the king does not give up setting himself apart as the wise one, he will always be separated from his subjects, separated by the dualistic barrier and unable to communicate from the heart. There is enlightenment, Rinpoche says, **but there is still a king and his subjects and they must run the world together. Running the world becomes an expression of sanity because there is no reference point against which to fight.** Enlightened beings are able to enter into all six realms of samsara—from the hell realm to the god realm—without hesitation and work with the situation as it is, without struggle.

I'm sure that sentient beings caught in the madness of samsaric habitual patterns, with no idea how to help themselves, seem pretty crazy to bodhisattvas and fully awakened beings. But this awakens their compassion and tenderness rather than their scorn. Their passion is to help in any way possible.

I've always admired how Rinpoche joined right in with our wild hippie world. In Tibet he had been the head of Surmang Monastery and was always given great respect and special treatment. When I met him for the first time, at a hippie commune in northern New Mexico, he was sleeping on the floor next to the three men who had come with him from Boulder. He was barefoot and wearing blue jeans and made a point of not being anyone special. This made a great impression on me.

I talk about this first meeting in my foreword to *The Myth of Freedom*. It was 1972, and I was teaching eight- to twelve-year-old children at an alternative elementary school in Taos, New Mexico. My life had already begun to change, thanks to reading Rinpoche's *Garuda* magazine article about working with negativity, and I felt inspired to read my pupils his memoir, *Born in Tibet*. The children were intrigued by the book and wanted to meet Rinpoche, so I had them write him letters.

Not long after, I received a reply from John Baker, one of the editors of *The Myth of Freedom*, saying that Rinpoche would soon be teaching at a commune near us and that we were invited to come visit him. When we arrived at the commune, one of his students came to tell us that Rinpoche wanted the children to know that we shouldn't make a big deal about him or glorify him in any way. This set the stage for a wonderful first encounter. The children gave him gifts and asked him many questions, and I had met my teacher.

Rinpoche acted in a way that bridged the gap between himself and his students. He often taught about not feeling that the teacher is higher and you're lower—not getting an inferiority complex about the relationship. He consciously did things so as not to come across as an OM-chanting holy man who transcended ordinary experience. It seems to me that he intentionally did things to try to get himself off the pedestal. For instance, he started to smoke cigarettes. But it wasn't so easy to get off the pedestal because the students admired and respected him so much. When he started smoking, everybody started smoking. And when he stopped, the outcome was predictable: Everybody stopped.

The ten bhumis are ten stages of gradually learning how to help others and the world: from the first-bhumi, irreversible, fully stabilized experience of shunyata to the post-tenth-bhumi experience of awakening, the experience called Buddhahood. It's a process of shedding shenpa, shedding our image, our binary thinking, the veils that obscure the fundamental openness of our mind and heart. It's a process of letting go of the acknowledger and relaxing into big-sky mind. Yet all along it's been a journey without goal, without any idea of achievement—a journey, as Suzuki Roshi would say, with "no gaining ideas."

Rinpoche summarizes the bodhisattva's journey through the ten bhumis. **At the beginning of the bodhisattva path,** by which he means the first bhumi, **there is the tremendous joy of realizing that we have all kinds of richness and skill, that we are a total human being.** Because we have such confidence in our richness, we can give and give and give. There is no sense of poverty, nothing to obscure us, nothing to hinder us from being **a total human being.**

Beyond that level, he continues, **the journey is not self-conscious, but still the unself-consciousness becomes another kind of self-consciousness. We are still using reference points, in a transcendental way of course, but we are nevertheless confirming our experience. And then, beyond the seventh bhumi, we begin to break through this barrier by experiencing complete skillful means.**

Bodhisattvas at this level can go into the most extreme suffering and stay open without getting triggered. Or even if they do get triggered, they can still keep their hearts and minds open to those who are suffering. They can go into hell and be of benefit. They can be a light in the darkness because they themselves don't get swept away.

Finally, Rinpoche says, **we do not have to make a reference, we do not have to make a journey at all.** This **leads into the tenth bhumi . . . the development of the paramita of** ***yeshe***, or nonconceptual wisdom. And beyond that? Full awakening, here we come!

Q&A

Q: I get confused around this issue of becoming a bodhisattva and making meaning for yourself in that way. I'm a recovering Catholic and have murky concepts about martyrs and saints, which can get confused with not knowing how to care for yourself. There's also the issue of using this path to avoid myself. I can be so busy making sure that other people are being attended to or cared about. It's genuine, but then it surpasses me taking the time to know myself.

PEMA: This is what the therapist and writer John Welwood refers to as "spiritual bypassing." You could use the bodhisattva path to enable tendencies like letting people walk all over you, or whatever it might be. We don't want to use these teachings to strengthen unhealthy patterns.

That's why this is taught as a step-by-step process, where the first step is making friends with yourself. That doesn't mean you don't help people. But it means that to the degree that you have an unconditional friendship with yourself, to that degree you'll have an unconditional friendship with other people. Otherwise, your main motivation for helping others could be to make yourself feel better. You can tell that's the case because of how you feel when no one thanks you. You don't feel so great.

Rather than having an ideal about being a bodhisattva, put that aside and let the journey evolve naturally. Instead of having ideals, work on unconditional friendship with yourself. If you're naturally a giving person, keep doing that. If you develop this unconditional friendship gradually, over the course of five years or so—and if you keep rereading *The Myth of Freedom* so you have no misunderstandings about what Rinpoche has to say about making friends with oneself—then you'll begin to see your patterns so clearly that you'll be able to set boundaries. You'll know when enough is enough. You'll know when you're not really helping the other person but enabling them to continue doing something unhealthy. You'll also know your limits and be able to decline requests for help, knowing that it's time to rest and refresh yourself in order to continue helping in the future.

SEVEN

DEVOTION

SURRENDERING

RINPOCHE DEDICATES a whole chapter to the often controversial subject of devotion. Devotion to whom? And for what reason? And is it really necessary? In this chapter, he delves into these questions thoroughly, covering them in five sections: "Surrendering," "Spiritual Friend," "The Great Warrior," "Commitment," and "The Universality of Guru."

Many of us would rather just read books or listen to recordings and forget about having a teacher. But from my personal point of view and training, studying on our own can only take us so far. This is because we tend to keep recycling everything we read or hear through what we already believe. A discussion with other people can at least challenge our views and opinions, and a teacher whom we fully trust can do that even more. For me, the relationship with the teacher—as well as with the sangha—is crucial in terms of waking up.

Although devotion is not emphasized much in Zen, nor in the Buddhist meditation that comes from Burma, it is central to the Buddhism that went to Tibet, usually referred to as vajrayana. This is the Buddhism that I've been connected with for over forty years, so the topic is an important one for me. In the vajrayana, working with the teacher is considered the fast path to shedding your ego. You can go a long, long way in a relationship with the teacher.

The first aspect of devotion that Rinpoche addresses is *surrendering.* **In order for you to make friends with a teacher in a complete sense,** he says, **he or she has to know what you are and how you are. Revealing that is surrendering.** In other words, the core of devotion to a teacher, the key to surrendering, is trusting the teacher enough to let them see us. Letting all our negativity, selfishness, and shame be seen takes courage. We need to develop the ability to be vulnerable without crawling back into our cocoon. I have found from personal experience that this requires time.

The main obstacle to developing such trust, Rinpoche says, is low self-esteem. This is the feeling of not measuring up, of being inadequate—what he calls earlier in the book **poverty mentality**. Entering the student-teacher relationship with this feeling is extremely common. When we respect and admire someone so much that we regard them as our teacher—and even ask them formally to be in this role—we tend to put them on a pedestal and regard ourselves as lesser: "The wise one is exalted, and I am the neurotic one needing help."

In my experience, and having explored this subject with others, the student initially can't help putting the teacher on a pedestal, even when the teacher warns them not to. I once implored a student, "Please, you've got to get me off the pedestal." But doing this is not so simple, even if the student understands intellectually that it's an obstacle.

The more inadequate they feel, Rinpoche says, **the more devoted they become. The poorer you feel, the richer the guru seems by contrast.** This attitude is based on feeling flawed. We see ourselves as **a miserable little person who is being given a golden cup, then we are overwhelmed by the gift, we do not know what to do with it**. The teacher wants to share the teachings and practices, but we're not sure if we're worthy of receiving them.

On the other hand, your devotion may not come from feeling inadequate. You may feel there is no gap between you and your beloved teacher. Your gratitude is unconditional and heartfelt. But in this case, Rinpoche suggests that we ask ourselves what we want in return for our devotion: **Before we wholeheartedly give ourselves to serving a guru, we should be very suspicious of why we are doing it. What are we looking for, really?**

If you enter the relationship hoping to be saved from pain and problems—essentially hoping not to have to be who you are—then true awakening will be impeded. The foundation of devotion has to be your willingness to be who you are, just as you are. Honesty with the teacher is based on honesty with yourself. Rinpoche says, **If your movements are clumsy or if your hands are dirty when you shake hands, you should not be ashamed of it. Just present yourself as you are.**

Rinpoche taught that we have to be willing to see our neuroses as neuroses. As a student who has worked closely with several teachers, I know how hard that is. Being in the presence of the teacher is a special situation that brings out your best behavior. But for the relationship to have the intended effect, best behavior can be problematic because the teacher might think that you actually have no neuroses. The teacher may have to snoop around and ask other people what they observe. Maybe the student bites people's heads off and explodes all the time, but the teacher never gets to see that. It's important, however, that sooner or later, the teacher does get to see it, and that the student gets to see the teacher as well, so no one is holding anything back. It's a two-way street.

Rinpoche says that the relationship with the teacher is similar to the doctor-patient relationship: **You must tell your doctor what is wrong with you, what symptoms you have. If you tell the doctor all your symptoms, then he or she can help you as much as possible. Whereas if you try to hide your illness, try to impress the doctor with how healthy you are, how little attention you need, then naturally you are not going to receive much help.**

Smiling all the time and trying to get approval and confirmation blocks openhearted communication with the teacher. It hinders a deeper connection. The problem with low self-esteem is that every time our flaws get exposed, we feel we've messed up—and that there's something fundamentally wrong with us. It's too threatening to be seen that clearly. We retreat and put up our shield. We're no longer able to contact our own heart and our own wisdom. In this condition, it's impossible to receive much from our teacher. We are like a cup with a lid. Nothing can get in, and this is sad. So, making friends with ourselves is the foundation of a true friendship with the teacher.

When you feel like you can trust your teacher's motivation, that's when you're ready to be "messed with." Usually the teacher knows instinctively when students are ready. They don't mess with a student in order to mess them up but because they see that some rugs need to be pulled out for the student to go further in the process of awakening. In this relationship, a spiritual teacher is willing to use all the means at their disposal to help the student wake up, and the student is receptive even when it's painful.

We may fear that if we surrender, we'll become like a follower of Jim Jones, who ordered nine hundred people in his cult to drink cyanide-laced Kool-Aid. But for Rinpoche, "surrendering" means doing what it takes to let go of our habitual self-centeredness. This letting go is fundamental to the teacher-student relationship.

Rinpoche describes the process of surrendering our self-importance as like becoming part of a huge stew. This is similar to the notion of being a grain of sand. **Everybody jumps into a gigantic cauldron,** he says. **It does not matter how or when you jump into it, but sooner or later you must**—that is, if you want to shed your armor and have open communication with yourself and with the world. **The water is boiling, the fire is kept going. You become part of a huge stew. The starting point of devotion is to dismantle your credentials,** to dismantle your ego-clinging, your self-centeredness. In other words, you have to let go of hoping that the relationship will give you ground and be another feather in your cap.

He continues, **You need discoloring, depersonalizing of your individuality. The purpose of surrender is to make everyone gray—no white, no blue—pure gray.** (Now, this may not sound too attractive!) **The teaching demands that everyone be thrown into the big cauldron of soup. You cannot stick your neck out and say, "I'm an onion, therefore I should be more smelly." "Get down, you're just another vegetable." "I'm a carrot, isn't my orange color noticeable?" "No, you are still orange only because we haven't boiled you long enough."**

He goes on: **At this point you might say to yourself, "He's warning me to be very suspicious of how I approach the spiritual path, but what about questioning him? How do I know that what he is saying is true?" You don't. There is no insurance policy. In fact, there is much reason to be**

highly suspicious of me. You never met Buddha. You have only read books that others have written about what he said. Assuming that Buddha knew what was true, which of course is itself open to question, we do not know whether his message was transmitted correctly and completely from generation to generation. Perhaps someone misunderstood and twisted it. And the message we receive is subtly but fundamentally wrong.

How do we know that what we are hearing is actually trustworthy? Perhaps we are wasting our time or being misled. Perhaps we are involved in a fraud. There is no answer to such doubts, no authority that can be trusted. Ultimately, we can trust only in our own basic intelligence.

This last sentence is important enough for me to repeat, and for all of us to keep in mind continually as we follow the spiritual path: **Ultimately, we can trust only in our own basic intelligence.**

If we have doubts about a teacher's motivations, then we need to examine that teacher carefully. As our courage grows, we can do this more and more thoroughly until we are satisfied. In my relationships with Trungpa Rinpoche and Dzigar Kongtrul Rinpoche, I tried to get as close to them as I could to make sure I could fully trust them—not to fulfill all my wishes and do everything on my terms but to have my best interests at heart.

As your commitment grows, you find that your devotion, especially in the vajrayana, is not really to a human being but to awakening. You become more committed to shedding your ego, more motivated to awaken for the benefit of sentient beings. The teacher is a doorway to this process, but you have to do it yourself. The teacher's job is to help you connect with your own intelligence about what's strengthening and what's self-destructive, what's on the path and what's off the path. But you can only awaken by yourself. There's no other way.

Having made this commitment, when the teacher or anything else in the world triggers you, you're more apt to stay open and catch your habitual responses when they start to click in. Your clear intention makes you less prone to scramble for ground immediately. You become more willing to be vulnerable, more eager to have the bubble of ego popped. At the same time, you accept that sometimes you will fail. As Dzigar Kongtrul Rinpoche says, "Failing isn't a problem as long as we don't give up."

This up-and-down process is the beginning of truly surrendering. But until the rug is pulled out, despite ourselves, we want the relationship to confirm us, to give us ground, to bolster us up. So when the relationship is not doing that anymore—hip, hip, hooray!

Trungpa Rinpoche gives guidelines for determining whether our relationship with the teacher is genuine: **Your first impulse might be to look for a one-hundred-percent enlightened being, someone who is recognized by the authorities, who is famous, who seems to have helped people we know. The trouble with that approach is that it is very difficult to understand what qualities an enlightened being would have. We have preconceptions as to what they are, but do they correspond to reality?**

What he stresses is that the relationship has to be **based upon our personal experience of communication with this person, rather than upon whether or not the person fits our preconceptions**. For a teacher-student relationship to go deeper, there needs to be a heart-to-heart connection. This doesn't mean that you call each other on the phone or sit up all night talking. You may rarely see or speak to your teacher. But whenever you can, you let yourself be seen as fully as possible. As your trust in the relationship grows, you feel more and more trust that you can share yourself honestly.

Dzigar Kongtrul Rinpoche said that for years he thought his teacher Dilgo Khyentse Rinpoche disapproved of him. Hearing this reminded me of thinking the same about my own teachers—Trungpa Rinpoche, Kongtrul Rinpoche, and others. But Kongtrul Rinpoche eventually understood that, in fact, he was the one who disapproved of himself. His heightened neurosis in the presence of his teacher had more to do with his own thoughts than about his teacher's.

This heightened neurosis is what makes you feel so uncomfortable and ill at ease with the teacher. It's as if you're always on a first date with someone you strongly hope will like and admire you. In this state, it's not unusual to hide all kinds of things; and even if you're trying to be open and show yourself to the teacher, you feel as if you're covered in pimples and have bad breath. In the end, Kongtrul Rinpoche realized that his teacher didn't disapprove of him at all. His teacher accepted both his confusion and his wisdom—and he wanted to see even more of the confusion in order to be of help.

The question to ask yourself is, "Do I have the courage to really show myself?" You could do so by honestly saying, "I hardly ever meditate" when you'd rather just hope that they think you meditate all the time. Teachers often will ask you to show yourself a little bit more, for example, by asking you to write about your life or send them your practice records. If you don't want to be seen, requests like these may provoke some resistance.

Something very special can happen in a close relationship with a teacher. Your mind and heart soften, and you connect with the best of yourself. When you're around your teacher or listening to their teachings, there's a sense of receiving something very ancient and precious, something infinite—traditionally referred to as *blessings*. The blessings of the teacher's lineage, which go back and back in time—all the way back to the time of the Buddha—cause you to go beyond your usual self-reference and self-preservation.

Rinpoche describes the fruition of surrendering in this way: **In the case of genuine friendship between teacher and student, there is direct and total communication which is called "the meeting of the two minds." The teacher opens and you open; both of you are in the same space.** In *Cutting Through Spiritual Materialism*, Rinpoche says, "This is the real way of uniting the blessing or *adhishthana*, the spiritual essence of the guru, and your own spiritual essence. The external teacher, the guru, opens himself or herself and, because you also are open, because you are 'awake,' there is the meeting of two elements which are identical." Sometimes this is poetically referred to as "pouring water into water." The teacher's mind and the student's mind aren't separate. Ultimately they share that vast space, that infinite great expanse, which is always right here.

SPIRITUAL FRIEND

BEGINNING WITH this section, Rinpoche describes three ways of relating to one's teacher: as a good parent, as a spiritual friend, and as a vajra master. All three are legitimate, powerful ways of benefiting from a connection to a teacher.

Many people have no wish to work with a teacher at all, but of those who do, almost everyone enters at the level where the teacher is like a parental figure. We have a gentle relationship with this teacher, whom we regard as a sane, reasonable person we can trust, much as we would trust a good parent. Rinpoche calls this the **hinayana Buddhist approach to devotion [where] you are confused and need to relate to a model of sanity, to a sensible human being who . . . sees the world clearly**. For many of us, this foundational level is deeply satisfying and it's where we choose to stay.

With the second way of relating to the teacher, the ante gets upped a bit. Here we consider the teacher from the mahayana view, as a **spiritual friend**. We relate to him or her as we would to a skilled physician. This physician has the skill of understanding and treating ego-clinging and neuroses. If we are looking for this kind of help, we are willing to follow their instructions.

The third way requires the most courage. When we're ready, we begin to experience our teacher as a great warrior, vajra master, or crazy-wisdom guru. This is the vajrayana approach, which I will talk about in the next section.

As we deepen our willingness to learn from a teacher, the more flexibility and open-mindedness we have, the more the teacher can help us. Generally, we begin with the hinayana relationship and build on that stable foundation. However, our process doesn't have to follow a strict, three-yana sequence. At different times, we may relate to the teacher in any of the three ways. As Rinpoche says in a later section, **One minute you might need a parental figure, another minute you feel sick and need a physician, another minute you might need warriorlike encouragement.** Still, Rinpoche warns against ambitiously jumping in and trying immediately to work with a vajra master. If we think that working with a vajra master is where it's at, and we want to skip the part about creating a good foundation, that won't work. In fact, it would be foolish and even dangerous.

In "Spiritual Friend," Rinpoche focuses on relating to the teacher as a skilled physician, saying that **we have to open ourselves to the suggestions of the spiritual friend at this point; he or she begins to mind our business a great deal**.

I often hear students talking about how they want the teacher to mind their business. They would like the teacher to point out their blind spots. But the first time the teacher gives them feedback, they wince and think they're probably with the wrong person.

Being open to the teacher's feedback can be hard. Receiving it can feel too embarrassing and painful. The main reason most of us can't see our blind spots is that we don't want to see them. Unless we are truly open to the teacher minding our business, it's best not to ask them to do so. If we're not ready for an answer we don't want to hear, then it's more skillful not to ask.

Over the years, I gradually developed a conviction that the main reason Rinpoche did anything with any of his students was to help us wake up. I learned this by watching how he related to people. I saw that he never gossiped about anyone, he never gave up on anyone, he stuck with you through thick and thin. I felt that I wasn't going to be an exception to the rule.

As Rinpoche says in the previous section, when you go to the doctor, you don't pretend that you're well. You have to let the doctor see what is wrong. And when the doctor gives you the medicine for your illness, you have to take it and not say, "No way am I taking this. I prefer my own remedies."

In his book *Fearless Simplicity*, Tsoknyi Rinpoche talks about the difficulty of reaching a level of commitment where the teacher can give you honest feedback. He humorously compares a student's approach to their path to a person "who comes to me with a cup containing water, ten spoonfuls of sugar, ten spoonfuls of chili, ten spoonfuls of oil, and many other things all mixed into a big mess. He says, 'Rinpoche, this doesn't taste good. I want it to taste better. Can you do something?' I say, 'Sure, I'll try.' And I start to pour some of the water out. The person jumps up and yells, 'Oh, please, don't pour any water out! I refuse to take anything out.' Wondering what I should do, I ask, 'Can I add more sugar?' Again he objects, 'No, no, I don't want to change anything—just make it taste good. I don't want to change anything except the taste.'"

If the student isn't willing to let go of anything, there's nothing a teacher can do. To the degree that we as students are willing to let go of having everything on our terms, to that degree we can receive feedback and see our blind spots.

As I've said, one of the blockages to relating to the teacher comes from feeling inadequate while romanticizing the teacher as perfect. Instead of helping us grow up, this makes us more infantile, and it prevents the teacher from being able to guide us.

I once heard Dzigar Kongtrul Rinpoche say, "Sometimes people sit in the front row and look at me like this." Here he made a comical face of intense devotion. When teachers see that gaze, they know that everything they say and do will be seen through the student's filter of perfection. When my daughter saw a group of women looking at me that way, she said, "Mom, I sure hope you don't buy that adulation cult stuff."

I heard that Kongtrul Rinpoche once said to a student who had that intensely devoted look, "Just move. I can't stand that look." A teacher would only speak like that to a student who had at least entered the physician level of the relationship. I'm sure Kongtrul Rinpoche would put up with the devoted gaze of a student who saw him as a "good parent" because at that level they might be too fragile and easily hurt. But more seasoned students have more resilience to hang in there. This gives the teacher the freedom to say, "I can't stand that look." It's not really about the teacher being bothered. The teacher is addressing adulation and how it can be an obstacle to the student's path.

As Trungpa Rinpoche said in "Buddhadharma without Credentials," the teacher shouldn't have "idiot compassion," and the student shouldn't have "idiot faith." There has to be intelligence on both sides: The teacher has to develop "intelligent compassion," and the student has to develop "intelligent devotion."

Rinpoche ends this section provocatively by saying that **the real function of a spiritual friend is to insult you**. This doesn't mean they tell you you're ugly. It means that as your courage and willingness to stop hiding increases, the teacher's feedback can become more direct and penetrating, and your progress can happen more quickly.

THE GREAT WARRIOR

THIS MAY BE the most challenging section of the book. Here Rinpoche begins to talk about the vajrayana teacher. Although he taught at all three levels mentioned in this chapter—the good parent, the skilled physician, and the great warrior—the great warrior, or vajra master, can only begin to manifest when the student's commitment is strong enough. No one pushes you into this kind of relationship, and no one demands it of you. It's something that happens because of your deepening commitment to sanity and your longing to shed all your credentials—to be without armor, to be completely open and receptive to the world, without shutting down into biases and prejudice every time you're provoked. You feel that the vajra master, male or female, offers the fastest path for doing this.

Up to this point, **your relationship was sympathetic, friendly, predictable. When you visited your friend he would always sit in the same chair and you would always be served the same kind of tea.** But when this becomes too predictable, you may begin to take it for granted. So next time you go to an interview expecting the usual seating arrangement, the teacher is sitting in your chair, and it throws you off.

I had an interesting situation like this once. I was at one of Rinpoche's three-month retreats and was working closely with him because I was head of practice and study. We met often, always in his sitting room. He would sit in his chair, and I and the other teachers would sit on the couch, and we would talk about what was going on in the retreat.

Then, at one point, I asked to speak with him about the founding of Gampo Abbey, our monastery in Nova Scotia. To my surprise, I heard back that he'd see me right away. This was unusual, so I was immediately caught off guard. I went up, expecting to be shown into the sitting room, but instead I was shown into his dimly lit bedroom.

He was sitting in bed, looking like he had just woken up. He had me come over and sit in front of him on the floor, and he proceeded to give me all the instructions about how to establish our monastery. To say that I was unnerved by the situation is an understatement.

A lot of things like that happened with Rinpoche, but I never felt that he contrived the situation, that he thought it up ahead of time and was trying to shock me. Probably he just wanted to talk about the monastery and hadn't gotten out of bed yet. At the same time, by being with him in that situation, I got the message that he didn't want a moralistic and uptight monasticism. At least, that was how I interpreted it. But the actual content of the meeting was simply Rinpoche's clear advice about establishing Gampo Abbey. It was a very sane and practical meeting—a business meeting, really.

Your spiritual friend will sit in your chair and serve you beer instead of tea. You are confused, you feel as if the carpet had been pulled from under your feet. The regularity and predictableness of your relationship has been challenged. That is how the spiritual friend turns into a crazy-wisdom guru.

To be clear, the spiritual friend won't manifest as the crazy-wisdom guru before you have the right foundation for that relationship to be helpful. First, you have to even want to work with a teacher at this level. Second, you must have a strong foundation of loving-kindness toward yourself. Finally, you have to be convinced, from the bottom of your heart, that the teacher has no other motivation than to wake you up. You can't expect them to behave in a predictable way, but you trust their motivation. You also have to trust their skill in helping you wake up, which may far surpass anything you could imagine. If you have this trust, the teacher can manifest as the vajra master, and the relationship can speed up your path of awakening considerably.

When the vajrayana teacher starts behaving in ways that can help free you from even the most entrenched forms of ego-clinging, you may feel totally exposed. Nevertheless, you hang in there because you've gotten to a place where all you want is to have your propensities and well-entrenched habits exposed. You're aware of how painful it is when your deepest neuroses are revealed to you, but even so, you appreciate it greatly.

Rinpoche once asked a student (I'll call him "Joe") to do a project, but Joe approached it half-heartedly and never really got it going. Since Rinpoche didn't say anything, Joe figured he didn't mind the lack of progress. Then Rinpoche was meeting with some students, including Joe, and said, "I think we need to find somebody else to do the project. It's been two years and Joe must not have been able to find the time." He simply stated the facts without any harshness, but his plain words struck Joe like a lightning bolt. Although the experience was painful, Joe felt grateful to Rinpoche for awakening him from a dull and sluggish fog that he didn't even know had entrapped him.

When Rinpoche was alive, I knew there was nowhere I could hide. I valued that. Although it was extremely uncomfortable to see where I was artificial or people-pleasing or arrogant, that exposure was what I wanted. After Rinpoche died, despite my best intentions to stay honest with myself, I began to take other people's high opinions of me far too seriously. I began even to believe in their complete validity. After a while I realized that I badly needed someone who could blow my cover. Fortunately, I met Dzigar Kongtrul Rinpoche, who is a master at this.

There was a time, for instance, when Kongtrul Rinpoche encouraged me repeatedly to do more retreat at Samten Ling, his retreat center in Crestone, Colorado. I said that seemed impossible given my teaching schedule. Yet he kept encouraging me. Eventually I figured out how to rearrange my schedule, and I proudly told Kongtrul Rinpoche I could come to Samten Ling twice a year to do retreat.

Not long afterward, when my travel plans were neatly scheduled, he gathered a small group of us together and pointedly questioned our commitment and whether it was even worth his time to work with us. I felt exposed and uncomfortable. Then he looked directly at me and said, "Because of various changes we are making, I don't think we will have room just now for Ani Pema to do her retreats here."

I remember thinking that if I had tried to figure out a way that Kongtrul Rinpoche could help me see my neuroses, I would never in a million years have come up with this one. In one sentence he showed me my pride, my complacency, and my constant desire to be seen as a good student, the one who does everything right. I was totally floored. It was very painful, but I never doubted Kongtrul Rinpoche's desire to help me. I never doubted his motivation and care.

After this happened, I became even more determined to practice what Kongtrul Rinpoche had taught me. Curiously and fortunately, instead of collapsing, I became energized and continued my retreat practice in a friend's house in Crestone. All that I had learned about working with my mind and emotions came in very handy when I needed it most.

At the stage of the skilled physician, all your issues start to come out—your issues with feeling left out; with loneliness, hopelessness, worthlessness. The relationship with the vajra master, when you're ready for it, brings them out even further. Now you no longer want to hide behind your masks and disguises. You don't want to die with your habitual tendencies still ruling your life.

One must make a very direct and personal relationship with the guru, Rinpoche says, speaking here about the vajra master. **You might give twenty million dollars to your spiritual friend whom you love dearly, but that is not enough. You must give your ego to him or her. The guru must receive your juice, your vital fluid. It is not enough to give him or her your feathers or hair or nails. You have to surrender the real core of you, the juicy part. Even if you give everything you have—your car, your clothes, your property, your money, your contact lenses, your false teeth—it is not enough. How about giving yourself, you who possess all these things?**

He continues, **We might feel proud that we gave one of our fingers to our guru: "I cut off my ear as a gift to him," or "I cut my nose as an expression of devotion to him. I hope**

he will take it and regard it as a sign of how serious I am about the whole thing. And I hope he will value it because it means so much to me." To the crazy-wisdom guru such sacrifice is insignificant. By that time, the teacher already knows how committed you are, so no gift, including your nose, will impress him or her much, unless it's accompanied by letting go of self-importance.

Allen Ginsberg once said to Rinpoche something like, "You just keep drinking because of ego." Rinpoche replied, "And you just keep that beard and keep writing poetry because of ego." So Allen went out and cut off his beard and brought it back to Rinpoche. And Rinpoche said, "Allen, you'll have to do better than that."

It is as Rinpoche says at the end of this section: **If you hold anything back, your relationship will be false, incomplete, and both you and your guru will know it.**

COMMITMENT

I HOPE IT'S CLEAR by now that the commitment is not to the teacher alone. With devotion, what we're really committing to is opening our heart and shedding our ego. Devotion is infused with love and gratitude, and it softens us up so profoundly that we are able to contact the vastness and warmth of our true nature.

Here, however, Rinpoche leaves no doubt that although devotion to the teacher opens your heart, you can't expect the relationship to be on your terms. **You would like to obtain some kind of acknowledgement that your neuroses are a valid and a serious matter, that they should be included as part of the bargain of the spiritual unification of guru and student. But such a bargain cannot be made because your guru will not sign his name on the dotted line.**

He presents the guru as dangerous, not a person to be fooled with. My experience is that the guru *is* dangerous—dangerous to your ego. As he says, **You might bend the income tax laws or plead your way out of a fine for a traffic violation, but it is not so easy with spirituality.**

Then: **What I am trying to say is that devotion to a teacher involves tremendous consequences. . . . You are surrendering yourself, acknowledging that you have some kind of commitment. And if you go so far as to regard**

yourself as a student of spirituality, then you are not only siding with the goodness of the teaching but you are also embedding yourself into the soil of the teaching. Each time you fold your hands and bow, each time the teacher acknowledges your commitment, each time you light candles or incense at a shrine or sit in a meditation hall, you are rooting yourself more deeply. It is like planting a tree. Each time you water the plant, the roots grow further into the ground. Devotion is usually regarded as inconsequential. You bow and you get what you want. If you do not get it, you can walk away without any difficulty. ***Not so.***

Not so. The italics are not in the original, but I feel the need to emphasize those two words. It gets harder and harder to walk away because you know you're not just walking away from a person or an organization. You're walking away from what you know to be true: that all our pain comes from ego-clinging, and that in order to free ourselves from this deeply entrenched habit, we need help. Right now, to a greater or lesser degree, each of us knows this. The more you commit to wanting to be completely free, the harder it is to forget about this commitment as if you had never made it.

As Rinpoche says, **each bow creates a stronger umbilical cord** to sanity. **You become more deeply rooted in the teaching and more deeply rooted in the debt you have to repay to all sentient beings.** Our debt is not just to the teacher but to all sentient beings. He makes this explicit in his book *Journey without Goal*, when he says, "Even if we attain the state of liberation or openness, we still have debts, because the rest of our brothers and sisters in the world are still in trouble."

This entire section reads like a threat or a warning: **You cannot really leave without being touched. It is a terrible**

trap in that sense, an extraordinarily haunting thing. So realize what you are doing. That is the main message of "Commitment." Don't enter into this ego-shedding relationship naively. Be discerning and intelligent and **realize what you are doing.**

THE UNIVERSALITY OF GURU

WORKING WITH THE teacher is a step-by-step process. As Rinpoche writes, **Each stage along the path has its dominant themes. The hinayana approach is predominantly a simple relationship with your spiritual friend, a human relationship. Your spiritual friend is not regarded as a god, saint, or angel, but . . . as a human being who has gone through tremendous discipline and learning. We can identify with this person because we can communicate with him or her.** Here, even though he uses the term *spiritual friend*, he is referring to the teacher as a good parent.

The mahayana teacher, the skilled physician, is a person who **never gives up hope for you.** As an example of this level of patience and kindness, Rinpoche gives a funny and painfully accurate example of just how challenging it can be for a teacher to work with a student:

You do something wrong and he instructs you how to correct it. But then you slip up or distort the instruction; you create further mistakes. You go back to your spiritual friend and he says, "Fine, we can still work together, but now try this project," and you try again. You start with tremendous energy and confidence that you can do it. Several days later you get tired of the whole thing. You find something else with which to entertain yourself. The spiritual

friend might ask you to do an intensive meditation practice without reading books, but you find that a book jumps into your lap and you cannot help reading it. It seems to be a part of the teaching as well. And you go back to the spiritual friend and say, "I followed your instructions but this book jumped into my lap and I could not help reading it." The spiritual friend then says, "That's fine. Did you learn anything from it? If you did, take the book and keep reading, find out what the book has to say in depth." And you go back and try to read the book, but you tire of reading. It's springtime. The flowers and trees and nature are so glamorous that you cannot help putting the book aside and taking a nice walk, enjoying the beauty of nature and the "meditative" state of being in nature.

It goes on like that. The teacher never gives up on you because sooner or later they know you're going to smell your own rat. Rinpoche describes the teacher at this level as **like a crocodile: once you land in its mouth it never lets you go.**

Rinpoche emphasizes not losing our sense of humor, not becoming **too serious.** Speaking of the same easily distracted student, he says, **Following discipline is very difficult and you constantly create sidetracks by not realizing that you are sidetracking. The problem is not that you disobey your spiritual friend. In fact, the problem is that you are too serious; you find your sidetracks by being very serious.** Instead of merely getting distracted, you take your distractions very seriously by justifying them. You don't just go for a nice walk; you regard it as **the meditative state of being in nature**, not even recognizing that you are sidetracking.

You may have a feeling of love and devotion for your spiritual teacher as good parent, skilled physician, or great warrior, but that alone is incomplete. As you can see from this example, for the instructions to really be beneficial, a student also needs to have some discipline.

The word *discipline* usually refers to ethical conduct, but here it also means a willingness to catch our ego-clinging and reactivity when they arise and to train in not biting the hook. As Rinpoche puts it, **It is important first to develop a sense of devotion that allows us to be disowned by our ego. Devotion is a process of unlearning.** By "disowned" I take him to mean that we are no longer dominated—or "owned"—by our ego. What does he mean by "unlearning"? This means returning to the wide-open, unbiased beginner's mind—a mind not cluttered with preconceptions, fixed views, and opinions that keep us from seeing with fresh eyes.

The hinayana and mahayana approaches lay the necessary foundation for the vajrayana type of devotion. **We cannot begin immediately with the vajrayana devotional approach,** Rinpoche warns. **It would be suicidal.**

In this chapter on devotion, the vajrayana guru has thus far been presented as a highly evolved person who uses any means necessary to help you shed your confusion and connect with your wisdom. This person is willing to upset your applecart, to do anything they can to help you leave your self-important, ego-clinging ways behind.

In "The Universality of Guru," Rinpoche takes devotion even further and describes how **the phenomenal world becomes an expression of the guru**. You reach a point where there's a sense of devotion not just to a person or the teachings but to the world just as it is. All that occurs, all that you think, everything becomes an expression of the guru. This is a stage where **teachings are everywhere** and therefore **you can-**

not get away from this guru. In fact, he says, you don't want to get away because you've discovered that the phenomenal world itself will wake you up, and this becomes refreshing and wondrous. **Everyday events become self-existing teachings.**

Everything is your working basis. But you only arrive here because the teacher has been presenting you all along with a path of nonrejecting, a path of openness and receptivity to whatever might occur in your life. You only arrive here because ego is no longer getting in the way. You are no longer torturing yourself by succumbing to an ego-driven way of life.

The nondual view of being "one with" our experience, which Rinpoche has been discussing all along, is now described as **the all-pervading devotion in which the devotee is not separate from the object of devotion.** In his book *Notebooks of a Wandering Monk*, Matthieu Ricard tells of the instruction he received when he left his beloved teacher Kangyur Rinpoche for the first time. "Keep your teacher constantly in mind," he was told. "Merge your mind with his and he will never be apart from you." That's the idea here.

As I discussed earlier, at the level of the first bhumi, bodhisattvas have a direct, complete, and irreversible experience of seeing everything just as it is. They see without conceptual overlay. Then, while progressing through the ten bhumis, they develop the skillful means to communicate this realization to others. Traditionally it is said that the path through the ten bhumis takes one "countless eon" to traverse. But with the vajrayana, it's taught that for a very dedicated practitioner like the famous twelfth-century yogi Milarepa, it is possible to accomplish the entire path—from where we are now to enlightenment—in one lifetime. Even if you aren't close to being Milarepa, it is said that you can still attain enlightenment within three lifetimes. Of course, you don't know which lifetime you're in now. Are you in the first, the second, or the third? You'll never know.

However, we have to start where we are and not jump ahead of ourselves. In my opinion, the best approach to take is that of the "journey without goal": just using this moment right now to wake up and not focusing on what we may or may not experience in the future. It's just now, now, now.

Q&A

Q: Did Trungpa Rinpoche find it especially frustrating or challenging to teach Buddhism to Westerners?

PEMA: He loved teaching Buddhism to Westerners. When he came to the United States, he felt like he had hit the jackpot. There was this wild, untamed energy and no preconceptions to speak of, but a big appetite for spirituality. He did feel it was misguided toward spiritual materialism and that many students thought they were superior to people with routine, regular kinds of lives. All of that he had to work with, but he loved the Western students and he thrived on teaching us. He referred enthusiastically to his work as "taming untamable beings."

EIGHT

TANTRA

ALONENESS

Rinpoche starts this section with a warning: **The spiritual path is not fun—better not to begin it.** Reading this as a new student in 1977 didn't stop me in my tracks and cause me to think twice. In fact, it had the opposite effect. It drew me in.

For one thing, I wasn't really looking for "fun." I was very confused and unhappy, but what I resonated with was the teaching that my pain wasn't really a problem as long as I stayed with the immediacy of the experience and didn't try to escape it. So when I read, **If you must begin, then go all the way, because if you begin and quit, the unfinished business you have left behind begins to haunt you all the time,** I thought, "That makes sense to me, and I'm eager to get into this fully."

Looking back on this now, I see Rinpoche's words as an admonition not to start this path in a superficial way. Don't begin with the attitude of "I'll try this for a while, and if it doesn't suit me, I'll just leave and try something else." At some point, when a path is really ringing true and you feel trust in a teacher and the teachings, it's time to stick to one boat and let your experience deepen.

This kind of warning is meant for students who have already meditated for some time and have looked intelligently and open-mindedly at the organization, at the other students, and at the teacher. It's directed at students who already feel they've found something that touches them. On the other hand, a certain amount of "spiritual shopping," as Rinpoche called it, is necessary in the beginning because you need to find what's a good fit. It's important to take classes and listen to teachings and go to retreats with various groups until something clicks.

Rinpoche once said that you should choose the tradition that seems most trustworthy to you and go deeper into it for at least five years. But if you just go from one thing to another because nothing satisfies, you stay on the surface and nothing penetrates. You never get to the point of having your ego addressed because you stay in the safe territory of your comfort zone.

Paraphrasing Suzuki Roshi in *Zen Mind, Beginner's Mind*, Rinpoche says, **The path . . . is like getting on to a train that you cannot get off.** For quite a while, you *can* get off and try another teacher or another approach, and that's actually a good idea. The time comes, however, for you to stay on the train and **ride it on and on and on**. You have to go beyond wanting everything to be on your terms. Finally, it's time to let yourself be challenged, time to go for the stretch.

Rinpoche goes on to talk about the **continual growth** offered by this path: **The continuity of the path is expressed in the ideas of ground tantra, path tantra, and fruition tantra.** And what are these? Although this is a teaching on vajrayana Buddhism, the descriptions will sound familiar. **Ground tantra is acknowledging the potential that exists within you** (your buddha nature or basic goodness) and acknowledging that **your starting point** is **your confusion and pain**. Later, he restates this as **We accept our basic qualities.**

With path tantra, **we tread the path, which could be hot or cold, pleasurable or painful**. We acknowledge that we have what it takes and are **able to be fundamentally alone**.

Then he uses an expression mentioned earlier, an expression that made me extremely uncomfortable when I first heard it: **You are willing to have an operation without the use of anesthetics.** My understanding of this is that you are willing to go through the growing-up process of **opening on and on and on** without entertaining yourself, without distracting yourself. **You are willing to be a lonely person, a desolate person, are willing to give up the company of your shadow, your twenty-four-hour-a-day commentator who follows you constantly, the watcher.**

You are willing, if not always able, to stay present with the vulnerability and rawness of the growth process without looking for alternatives. As he puts it, **quite possibly there is no such thing as spiritual practice except stepping out of self-deception**. There is no practice except unmasking, unlearning, coming back again and again to what's happening right now without pretending it's other than what it is.

Fruition tantra, he says, **is when we discover our basic nature**, which he has been pointing to from the first chapter. When we're willing to undergo the operation without anesthetics, we get in touch with loneliness and the feeling of desolation: **It is like living among snowcapped peaks with clouds wrapped around them and the sun and moon starkly shining over them.** Most of us, he says, appreciate this beauty if we are camping, but if we move in and actually live among those snowcapped peaks as Milarepa did, it becomes extremely unnerving. We want to return to someplace where we feel at ease. We long for our usual comforts.

During my early retreats, I used to get so desperate for entertainment that I would eagerly read the newspapers I'd gathered for lighting the woodstove, all of which were over six months old. I'd often feel as if I were living in a black-and-white world. When someone came to check on my meditation, it felt like technicolor entering. Once when Kongtrul Rinpoche visited my retreat cabin, I told him that if I had to keep looking at that same old tree out my window, day after day after day, I was going to scream. He told me to just keep meditating and that after a while that feeling would change. And he was right. Because I had no intention to leave the retreat, and I knew enough to just go through it with a minimum of wiggling and squirming, after a while I came to love that old tree.

In this process, which went on for years, I learned the importance of patience—patience with feeling what I feel even when it's very unwelcome. My experience of coming out the other side was one of deep contentment, no longer restless and agitated, just there alone. I was born alone, I'll die alone, and at least sometimes, I could be just fine with aloneness in between.

Rinpoche says that **it is possible to make friends with the desolation and appreciate its beauty**. This is when restless, agitated, "hot" loneliness becomes "cool" loneliness. This is when you settle down with yourself and your world without feeling the urge to bolt. **Great sages like Milarepa,** he says, **marry themselves to desolation, to the fundamental psychological aloneness. . . . Wherever they go they are alone, whatever they do they are alone. . . . Aloneness is**

there all the time. That aloneness is freedom, fundamental freedom, freedom from needing a hand to hold.

Aloneness is something you move toward slowly. It takes courage, and it takes time. It involves a process of getting accustomed to having no hand to hold. It's not just about having no people around. You can love solitude but not have any experience of aloneness. You can be alone in a mountain cabin busily writing a book or watching things on your computer or luxuriating in daydreaming.

But if you decide to put away all your devices and writing materials and books and simply be alone with yourself, meditating and letting your thoughts dissolve into space, then you likely will go through entertainment withdrawal.

As the Japanese poet Ryokan says, "If you want to find the meaning, Stop chasing after so many things." If you want to find fundamental freedom, settle down with yourself just as you are. Become familiar with staying present without sidetracks.

We can stay present with loneliness and desolation. When you feel the pull of wanting something—anything—to entertain you, something to hold on to, something to comfort you, see if you can resist that pull. If you don't let yourself get pulled off, then at some point, without your even noticing, you realize you are settled, content with just being. Having nothing to hold on to, Rinpoche says, **is a very big step toward true asceticism**. True asceticism isn't self-denial. It's the feeling of being just fine, just as you are. It's the feeling of being "happy for no reason," as Tsoknyi Rinpoche says.

Rinpoche once said that the ultimate way of making friends with loneliness is when we no longer seek comfort and security even from our discursive thoughts. This is inner,

true asceticism. We know the freedom that comes from not getting entangled in our internal chatter. We experience the total freshness and spaciousness of just being, not feeling the need to go elsewhere. In this state, **that aloneness or the space of desolation does not entertain you, does not feed you anymore**. You begin to realize that the word *desolation* is from ego's point of view. It's ego that is no longer being entertained or fed. It's as if we are emerging from a dark, smelly cocoon into the vast space and freshness of the mountain air.

This emerging has no conclusion. Rinpoche ends the section with these words: **The whole process is an endless odyssey. Having attained realization, one does not stop at that point, but one continues on, endlessly expressing buddha activity.** Endlessly, we keep doing all we can to alleviate the suffering of others.

Q&A

Q: I have felt a lot of loneliness come up when I go into retreat. Then it gets pretty neurotic: I get into how nobody likes me and how I'm always left out and things like that. Is it possible to feel loneliness without it becoming neurotic?

PEMA: The neurosis comes in with the storyline. That's the trick—to not buy into the storyline, whether it's feeling left out or any other mental chatter. Just let the feeling be what it is. Let it be natural energy, natural simplicity, just what it is, without it being called anything at all.

I learned this strongly once when I was overcome by loneliness at the painful end of a friendship. I happened to be in a cabin in rural Nova Scotia in November, practically at the end of the earth. My friend and I quarreled and when she left, the loneliness came up in a major way. I tried hard to get rid of it by calling people on the telephone. Everyone was sympathetic and offered kind advice, but the more people I talked to, the more my loneliness increased.

It was so deep, so penetrating, so primordial that I realized I had to be with it fully and that no one else could do this for me. Then I remembered these teachings and just felt the loneliness directly and compassionately until it gradually passed. Doing this, I stood in the shoes of everyone who had ever been lonely and felt that emotion's universal quality.

MANDALA

In this final section of the book, Rinpoche encourages us to take **a leap**. Instead of what he calls **a disciplined effort**—instead of having a strategy for how to proceed—we just leap. This is a daring and egoless thing to do, but it is necessary, he says, if we want to **relate to the universe more directly**. He's assuming, of course, that we would find that appealing.

First, Rinpoche revisits the theme of connecting with the energy of emotions, which he discussed in "Working with Negativity." (See page 103.) As I've said, the basic message of relating to energy directly—without avoiding it, without overthinking it, without "negative negativity"—made sense to me from the very first time I encountered Rinpoche's teaching on this subject. Ever since, this has been a major theme in my life and teachings.

Going through this process again and again has given me some inkling about what it means to become one with the energy of emotions. This term *one with* has appeared quite often in *The Myth of Freedom*. It's a way of talking about removing the dualistic barrier, a way of going beyond me here and the energy of emotions there, a way of expressing experientially what it feels like to dissolve the illusion of separateness. As Rinpoche puts it here, **One must transcend the**

ego's strategies—aggression, passion, and ignorance—and become completely one with those energies.

This is because aggression, passion, and ignorance are our go-to ways of avoiding feeling what we feel. They are the different styles in which we spin off, our exits from being fully present with the underlying energy. Rather than stay with that energy, we get angry and blame, we start craving and grasp, or we space out and shut down. When we don't get lost in any of those habitual ways, we can be here completely, one with our basic energy.

In "Working with the Emotions" (see page 95), Rinpoche stresses that becoming one with emotions is different from suppressing them or acting them out. As I quoted before, **the intelligent way of working with emotions is to try to relate with their basic substance, the abstract quality of the emotions, so to speak. The basic "isness" quality of the emotions. . .**

Understanding this experientially entails moving closer to the energy, softening to it rather than hardening against it. This is extremely counter-habitual, but it pays off. Habitually and automatically, we tense up and reject the intensity of emotions as if that will ease the pain. In fact, it's just the opposite. If we don't react against our emotions but contact their "isness," embrace them, and join with the energy, it eases our discomfort and the energy can pass through us. I've done this many times and know that it's possible. However, it takes a willingness to feel some pain initially and to soften to the edgy, panicky sensation that comes when we don't respond habitually.

Becoming familiar and relaxed with the energy of emotions in this way creates the causes and conditions for the energy to be transmuted. As I said in chapter 4, when you transmute the energy, its basic substance remains the same, but you experience it differently. Rinpoche writes that the transmutation of aggression, passion, and ignorance **is realized by practice of the father tantra, the mother tantra, and the union tantra. The father tantra is associated with aggression or repelling, the mother tantra is associated with seduction or magnetizing** or passion, and the union tantra is associated with ignorance. To actually do this practice, we once again follow the key instructions to not accept or reject our experience but to stay in the middle, to be totally present with whatever arises, free of views and opinions, bias and prejudice. Easier said than done, but this is the direction in which we are moving.

The essence of the practice is to contact the living energy of our emotions without filters—so directly that we experience their enlightened essence. With aggression or repelling, he says that **one experiences an energy that contains tremendous force. No confusion can enter it; confusion is automatically repelled.** He refers to this as **vajra anger**, or the indestructible or **diamondlike aspect** of energy. It is also called "mirror-like wisdom" because when the basic energy of anger is transmuted, we see clearly without distortion, as if looking into an unblemished mirror. Anger free of self-centeredness, free of the storyline of "me" and "my anger," is just energy.

In her book *Wisdom Rising*, Lama Tsultrim Allione says, "The state of mirror-like wisdom is, in fact, the very same energy that manifested as anger, but now the struggle is removed and the wisdom is revealed." She goes on: "If I am in a situation where anger is arising, I can find the clarity of anger when I release myself from the ego's habitual orientation toward the self and its relentless grasping." This is the key to transmutation—letting go of ego-clinging, releasing self-righteousness and strongly held views and opinions, and having to be right.

When the emotion of passion—also known as attachment, craving, seduction, addictive wanting, or fixating—arises, Rinpoche says that we find **a sane version of passion** by not grasping to **one particular highlight of a situation and ignor[ing] the rest of the area in which that highlight is located**. For instance, in a romantic relationship, we can become obsessed with the details of another person. All we can think of is what they look like, how they move or smile or speak. But this may be entirely based on what we need from them. We want them to desire us, to confirm us; we want to be attractive and seductive for them. In this process, we actually lose touch with who they are, how they may be feeling, what they may be needing. Neurotic craving, neurotic attachment is always about "me."

When you can experience passion without ulterior motives and needs, then you can view relationships of all kinds far more clearly. The sane aspect of attachment is called "discriminating awareness wisdom." You **welcom[e] every situation but with discriminating wisdom**. You can discriminate what's good for a whole situation rather than just what's good for "me."

To transmute ignorance into **all-pervading space** (or "dharmadhatu wisdom"), it's necessary to realize when we're feeling the dullness, depression, or denial of ordinary ignorance. Ignorance, along with passion and aggression, are traditionally referred to as the "three poisons" because they usually poison our well-being, our fundamental okayness. But instead of trying to get rid of these poisons, we move toward them and explore them. What is the texture of ignorance, of spaced-outness, of depression or dullness? What is its color? What does it feel like in our body? We touch it as best we can. We go deeper than our internal conversations. It is right here in our ordinary day-to-day ignorance, our ordinary spaced-outness, that we find the vastness of all-pervading space. We become one with this ignorance to discover its profundity.

I have a dear friend who has shown me both sides of ignorance—the wisdom side and the neurotic side—just by how she manifests. When she is self-absorbed, she manifests as spacy and disconnected; you could even say dissociated. She also seems grumpy and dissatisfied in a dull sort of way. But when ego gets out of the way, her energy becomes free-flowing and she rests easily, open to herself and the world. Her face appears relaxed, and there is a sense of ease and accommodation about her. She seems completely satisfied—satisfied to just be.

What's the difference between a neurotic emotion and its wisdom aspect? Rinpoche says that the latter prevails when there's no struggle. Elsewhere, he calls this lack of struggle "collaborating with reality."

The example he gave was familiar to anyone who had been through a Nova Scotia winter. You go out walking and the sleet and ice are lashing against your face. The automatic and completely futile reaction is to contract and resist the unpleasantness of the experience. But instead, you stop struggling and you collaborate. You soften to the experience, you relax into it. You stop talking to yourself about it, and guess what? The same experience minus the struggle becomes completely workable. When we collaborate with reality—specifically, when we collaborate with the energy of our emotions—then transmutation can occur. It's as straightforward as that.

The next topic he discusses, symbolism, took me a long time to understand experientially. Just as Rinpoche says in the first paragraph of this section, it requires taking **a leap**—a leap beyond mere intellectual understanding toward a direct, nonconceptual experience.

There are many ways of taking a leap, but in my case this nonconceptual experience came about through reading about symbolism in *Cutting Through Spiritual Materialism*:

> Symbol . . . is not a "sign" representing some philosophical or religious principle; it is the demonstration of the living qualities of what is. For instance, in the direct perception of a flower, the perception of naked insight, unclothed and unmasked, the color of the flower conveys a message over and beyond the simple perception of color.

This passage resonated deeply with an experience that was already familiar to me, the experience of perceiving the world without being lost in thought, without being caught in hope and fear. In meditation or otherwise, I'd had many experiences of a gap in the mental chatter. At those times, although they were still occasional, I had the sense of letting the world speak for itself. There was no need for my commentary.

Before finding this quote, when I would read something like **the symbolism inherent in what we perceive** or **understanding the vividness of the energy of the universe in terms of symbolism**, I had no idea what Rinpoche was talking about. The words didn't seem to connect with my experience even slightly. I was frustrated because I wanted to get to the bottom of what he meant and see its relevance to my life. When I fortuitously came across this quote, my understanding finally opened up. I realized that symbolism was not a distant, indecipherable concept but a way of perceiving reality—a way of perceiving that I had to some degree already experienced.

Most of the time, we're so caught up in our neuroses and mental chatter that there's no space in our minds to perceive things simply and directly. But, as he also says in *Cutting Through Spiritual Materialism*, when "conceptualized mind is not involved in the perception . . . we are able to see with great precision, as though a veil had been removed from before our eyes." This was my experience exactly.

In *Shambhala: The Sacred Path of the Warrior*, Rinpoche expresses symbolism without even using the word *symbolism*:

> Any perception can connect us to reality properly and fully. What we see doesn't have to be pretty, particularly; we can appreciate anything that exists. There is some principle of magic in everything, some living quality. Something living, something real is taking place in everything.

I hadn't been able to connect with the word *symbolism,* but these descriptions spoke to something I could feel, something alive, and the meaning of the word began to get through.

My favorite teaching on symbolism was an answer Rinpoche gave after one of his talks in the 1970s. A young woman raised her hand and asked him, "What is enlightenment like?" He sat up tall and beamed as he answered her: "It's like smelling tobacco or hearing a bugle for the very first time."

These discussions on working with energy, transmutation, and symbolism lead directly into the central theme of this final section of *The Myth of Freedom*: the mandala principle. As Rinpoche writes, **Complete union with the energy of the universe** [becoming one with it] **and seeing the relationships as well as the vividness of things as they are** [symbolism] **is the *mandala* principle.**

Mandala means "circle," both the center and the fringe. It has the sense of a sacred enclosure. In "The Way of Maha Ati," Rinpoche describes it like this:

> Learn to see everyday life as a mandala in which one is at the center, and be free of the bias and prejudice of past conditioning, present desires, and future hopes and expectations. The figures of the mandala are the day-to-day objects of one's life experience, moving in the great dance or play of the universe, the symbolism by which the guru reveals profound and ultimate meaning and significance. Therefore, be natural and spontaneous, accept and learn from everything.

In his book *Orderly Chaos*, Rinpoche talks about two kinds of mandala: the "samsaric mandala," in which ego is at the center, and the "buddha mandala," in which unfixated, egoless mind and heart are at the center. When self-absorption and neuroses are at the center, everything we experience is filtered through that narrow lens of bias and partiality. On the other hand, when egolessness is at the center—when we stand open to the energy of life—we discover a new way of seeing.

Rinpoche describes this in "The Way of Maha Ati" as follows:

> The everyday practice is simply to develop a complete acceptance and openness to all situations and emotions and to all people, experiencing everything totally without mental reservations and blockages, so that one never withdraws or centralizes into oneself.

A key question to ask ourselves is, "Right now, what is in the center of my mandala—my everyday, ongoing mandala?" In our everyday practice, sometimes we have a giant "me" at the center of our mandala. At other times, wisdom is at the center. We go in and out. Sometimes we perceive directly and without partiality, and sometimes we don't. When confusion is in the center, we perceive a confused world and behave in a confused way. But then we come back to being present with a clear mind. We come back to "nowness," seeing things just as they are, without our own version getting in the way.

This may happen for only a few seconds, but if we keep coming back to seeing the world without a storyline, then those few seconds can expand. Over time, "naked insight, unclothed and unmasked" will become more familiar. I feel like Rinpoche is giving us a sneak preview of how our path might unfold when he writes, **In the case of the tantric version of mandala, everything is centered around centerless space in which there is no watcher or perceiver. . . . There is no partiality in one's perspective.** He is describing here what it would be like to experience our life in an egoless, tender, and compassionate way.

He goes on to say, **Someone who is involved with a completely open attitude to the universe does not have to try to work these things out intellectually or even intuitively by**

effort, but the orders of the universe are obvious to him or her. Whatever he or she perceives speaks to him or her.

Then, introducing one of the central teachings in the vajrayana, he says, **Often it is said in the scriptures that all sight is the visual mandala, all sound is the mantra mandala, all thought is *chitta* mandala.** Here is how the great fourteenth-century sage Longchenpa expresses this view in his *Precious Treasury of the Basic Space of Phenomena*:

> Throughout the entire universe, all beings and all that manifests as form
> are adornments of basic space, arising as the ongoing principle of enlightened form.
> What is audible, all sounds and voices without exception, as many as there may be,
> are adornments of basic space, arising as the ongoing principle of enlightened speech.
> All consciousness and all stirring and proliferation of thoughts, as well as the inconceivable range of nonconceptual states,
> are adornments of basic space, arising as the ongoing principle of enlightened mind.

Rinpoche clarifies that the sacred view of "enlightened form" doesn't mean you see **deities dancing around**. It means you see this very room, this very space, this very life you live as sacred. "Enlightened speech" doesn't mean that you always hear **strange mantras echoing**. It means that sound itself wakes you from confusion. And when you say "enlightened mind," it doesn't mean you're having only holy thoughts or seeing **space with all sorts of psychic flashes**

occurring. It means that the movement of the mind is perfect just as it is.

When I first heard these teachings, I took them too literally and thought I must be missing something. Since I wasn't seeing deities or hearing mantras, I thought I must be doing something wrong, so it was a relief when Rinpoche brought these teachings more down to earth. Then I could begin to appreciate that enlightened form, sound, and mind are always right here, manifesting in everything I perceive. I began to understand that this itself was what it felt like to stand with an open heart, fully awake in the center of the mandala of life.

MAHAMUDRA UPADESA

THE MYTH OF FREEDOM concludes with Rinpoche's translation of an important tantric text by Tilopa, the eleventh-century founder of the Kagyu school, which was Rinpoche's principal lineage. *Mahamudra* is a Sanskrit word for the open, spacious mind that we come to know through meditation. *Upadesa*, also Sanskrit, is usually translated as "pith instruction," meaning a brief, practical instruction that points directly to the essence of whatever topic is being taught.

I'm not going to attempt to give a commentary on this beautiful poem, but I highly recommend reading through it slowly at least two or three times. In my experience, when you read such instructions by the great meditators of the past, it makes a positive imprint on your mind and plants a seed for a deeper understanding in the future. I also recommend reading *Tilopa's Wisdom*, an excellent book on this text by my beloved teacher Khenchen Thrangu Rinpoche.

One of the most accessible lines from the "Upadesa" relates to *The Myth of Freedom* as a whole: **If there is no rejecting or accepting, then you are liberated in the Mahamudra.** You are liberated into mind that is vast as space, mind that doesn't pick and choose. As Rinpoche has been saying all along, stay present with an open, curious, unfixated mind and experience whatever arises as the path to enlightenment.

The Myth of Freedom begins with the theme of fantasy and reality, in which Rinpoche emphasizes being **present, right here**. Now, with the pith instructions in Tilopa's poem, we find that we have come full circle. One of the central messages of the dharma, conveyed in countless teachings by the Buddha and his followers for over 2,500 years, comes down to this simple idea: Work with life just as it is.

Work with life just as it is. Work with your particular style of imprisonment just as it is. Work with your breath just as it is. Work with your emotions just as they are. Work with people just as they are. Work with your devotion just as it is. Work with the world just as it is.

If you do so, you'll find that, just as Rinpoche says in "Lion's Roar" (see page 97), **nothing is rejected as bad or grasped as good. But everything we experience in our life-situations, any type of emotion, is workable.**

APPENDIX

Basic Sitting Meditation

The technique of sitting meditation called shamatha-vipashyana (tranquility-insight) is like a golden key that helps us to know ourselves. In shamatha-vipashyana meditation, we sit upright with legs crossed and eyes open, hands resting on our thighs. Then we simply become aware of our breath as it goes out. It requires precision to be right there with that breath. On the other hand, it's extremely relaxed and extremely soft. Saying "Be right there with the breath as it goes out" is the same thing as saying "Be fully present." Be right here with whatever is going on. Being aware of the breath as it goes out, we may also be aware of other things going on—sounds on the street, the light on the walls. These things may capture our attention slightly, but they don't need to draw us off. We can continue to sit right here, aware of the breath going out.

But being with the breath is only part of the technique. These thoughts that run through our mind continually are the other part. We sit here talking to ourselves. The instruction is that when you realize you've been thinking, you label it "thinking." When your mind wanders off, you say to yourself, "Thinking." Whether your thoughts are violent or passionate or dull and sluggish; whether your thoughts are worried or fearful; whether your thoughts are spiritual thoughts, pleasing thoughts of how well you're doing, comforting thoughts, uplifting thoughts—whatever they are, without judgment or harshness simply label it all "thinking," and do that with honesty and gentleness.

The touch on the breath is light: Only about 25 percent of the awareness is on the breath. You're not grasping or fixating on it. You're opening, letting the breath mix with the space of the room, letting your breath just go out into space. Then there's something like a pause, a gap until the next breath goes out again. While you're breathing in, there could be some sense of just opening and waiting. It is like pushing the doorbell and waiting for someone to answer. Then you push the doorbell again and wait for someone to answer. Then probably your mind wanders off and you realize you're thinking again—at this point, use the labeling technique.

It's important to be faithful to the technique. If you find that your labeling has a harsh, negative tone to it, as if you were saying, "Dammit!"—that you're giving yourself a hard time—say it again and lighten up. It's not like trying to shoot down the thoughts as if they were clay pigeons. Instead, be gentle. Use the labeling part of the technique as an opportunity to develop softness and compassion for yourself. Anything that comes up is okay in the arena of meditation. The point is, you can see it honestly and make friends with it.

Although it is embarrassing and painful, it is healing to stop hiding from yourself. It is healing to know all the ways that you're sneaky; all the ways that you hide out or criticize people; all the ways that you shut down, deny, close off; all your weird little ways. You can know all that with some sense of humor and kindness. By knowing yourself, you're coming to know humanness altogether. We are all up against these things. We are all in this together. When you realize that you're talking to yourself, label it "thinking" and notice your tone of voice. Let it be compassionate and gentle and humorous. Then you'll be changing old stuck patterns that are shared by the whole human race. Compassion for others begins with kindness to ourselves.

The length of time you sit is up to you. It can be as short as ten minutes or as long as you like.

BIBLIOGRAPHY

Allione, Lama Tsultrim. *Wisdom Rising: Journey into the Mandala of the Empowered Feminine.* Atria/Enliven Books, 2018.

Kongtrul, Dzigar. *Diligence: The Joyful Endeavor of the Buddhist Path.* Shambhala Publications, 2024.

Kongtrul, Dzigar. *It's Up to You: The Practice of Self-Reflection on the Buddhist Path.* Shambhala Publications, 2006.

Kongtrul, Dzigar. *Peaceful Heart: The Buddhist Practice of Patience.* Shambhala Publications, 2020.

Longchen Rabjam. *The Precious Treasury of the Basic Space of Phenomena.* Translated by Richard Barron. Padma Publishing, 2001.

McLeod, Ken. *Reflections on Silver River: Tokme Zongpo's Thirty-Seven Practices of a Bodhisattva.* Unfettered Mind, 2014.

McLeod, Ken. *Wake Up to Your Life: Discovering the Buddhist Path of Attention.* HarperOne, 2002.

Nhat Hanh, Thich. *The Heart of the Buddha's Teaching: Transforming Suffering into Peace, Joy, and Liberation.* Harmony Books, 1999.

Patrul Rinpoche. *The Words of My Perfect Teacher.* Translated by the Padmakara Translation Group. Yale University Press, 2010.

Ponlop, Dzogchen. *Penetrating Wisdom.* Shambhala Publications, 2014.

Ricard, Matthieu. *Notebooks of a Wandering Monk.* MIT Press, 2023.

Shantideva. *The Way of the Bodhisattva.* Translated by the Padmakara Translation Group. Shambhala Publications, 2006.

Suzuki, Shunryu. *Zen Mind, Beginner's Mind: Informal Talks on Zen Meditation and Practice.* Shambhala Publications, 2011.

Thrangu, Khenchen. *Tilopa's Wisdom: His Life and Teachings on the Ganges Mahamudra.* Shambhala Publications, 2019.

Trungpa, Chögyam. *Born in Tibet.* Shambhala Publications, 2000.

Trungpa, Chögyam. "Buddhadharma without Credentials." Seminar. New York City, March 12, 1973.

Trungpa, Chögyam. *Cutting Through Spiritual Materialism.* Shambhala Publications, 2002.

Trungpa, Chögyam. *Journey without Goal.* Shambhala Publications, 2000.

Trungpa, Chögyam. *Meditation in Action.* Shambhala Publications, 2010.

Trungpa, Chögyam. *The Myth of Freedom and the Way of Meditation.* Shambhala Publications, 1976.

Trungpa, Chögyam. *Orderly Chaos: The Mandala Principle.* Shambhala Publications, 1991.

Trungpa, Chögyam. *The Path of Individual Liberation: The Profound Treasury of the Ocean of Dharma.* Vol. 1. Shambhala Publications, 2014.

Trungpa, Chögyam. *Shambhala: The Sacred Path of the Warrior.* Shambhala Publications, 2015.

Trungpa, Chögyam. "Things Get Very Clear When You're Cornered." In *The Collected Works of Chögyam Trungpa.*

Vol. 4, edited by Carolyn Rose Gimian. Shambhala Publications, 2004, 423-29.

Trungpa, Chögyam. *The Truth of Suffering and the Path of Liberation*. Shambhala Publications, 2010.

Trungpa, Chögyam. *Work, Sex, and Money.* Shambhala Publications, 1988.

Trungpa, Chögyam, and Rigdzin Shikpo. "The Way of Maha Ati." In *The Collected Works of Chögyam Trungpa*. Vol. 1, edited by Carolyn Rose Gimian. Shambhala Publications, 2003.

Tsoknyi Rinpoche. *Fearless Simplicity: The Dzogchen Way of Living Freely in a Complex World*. Rangjung Yeshe Publications, 2003.

RESOURCES

For information regarding meditation instruction or inquiries about a practice center near you, please contact one of the following:

Boulder Shambhala Center
1345 Spruce St.
Boulder, CO 80302
(303) 444-0190
boulder.shambhala.org

Drala Mountain Center
151 Shambhala Way
Red Feather Lakes, CO 80545
(970) 881-2184
dralamountain.org

Gampo Abbey
1533 Pleasant Bay Rd.
Pleasant Bay, Nova Scotia B0E 2P0
Canada
(902) 224-2752
gampoabbey.org

Halifax Shambhala Centre
1084 Tower Rd.
Halifax, Nova Scotia B3H 2Y5
Canada
(902) 420-1118
halifax.shambhala.org

Karmê Chöling
369 Patneaude Lane
Barnet, VT 05821
(802) 633-2384
karmecholing.org

Mangala Shri Bhuti, the Sangha of Dzigar Kongtrul Rinpoche
Ward, Colorado and Vershire, Vermont
mangalashribhuti.org

Naropa University
2130 Arapahoe Ave.
Boulder, CO 80302
(800) 772-6951
naropa.edu

The Pema Chödrön Foundation
pemachodronfoundation.org

ACKNOWLEDGMENTS

First and foremost, I would like to thank my beloved root guru, the Vidyadhara Chögyam Trungpa Rinpoche, for his continual inspiration throughout my life. I'd also like to thank my other teachers, in particular, Dzigar Kongtrul Rinpoche for his great kindness and his guidance in my practice.

I am grateful to the following people who helped bring this book to fruition. Gigi Sims transcribed the original talks I gave in Berkeley in 2007. My friend Barbara Abrams read a draft of this book and asked many good questions. Glenna Olmsted, in addition to the constant support she always gives me, read through this manuscript and offered valuable suggestions. Jenn Brown, our editor at Shambhala Publications, fine-tuned the writing with the help of project editor Breanna Locke, copyeditor Emily Wichland, and proofreader Karen Steib. Nikko Odiseos, the president of Shambhala Publications, oversaw the project while always keeping a big picture in mind.

Finally, I want to acknowledge the enormous help and support of my editor Joseph Waxman. The book was very much a collaboration between the two of us. It was a lot of fun and very interesting working with Joey. Because I was in retreat for much of the two years that we sporadically worked on the book, it took a lot of patience and flexibility on his part, and I greatly appreciate it. Thank you, Joey, for everything.

ABOUT THE AUTHOR

ANI PEMA CHÖDRÖN was born Deirdre Blomfield-Brown in 1936, in New York City. She attended Miss Porter's School in Connecticut and graduated from the University of California at Berkeley. She taught as an elementary school teacher for many years in both New Mexico and California. She has two children and three grandchildren.

While in her mid-thirties, Ani Pema traveled to the French Alps and encountered Lama Chimé Rinpoche, with whom she studied for several years. She became a novice nun in 1974 while studying with Lama Chimé in London. His Holiness the Sixteenth Karmapa came to Scotland at that time, and Ani Pema received her ordination from him.

Ani Pema first met her root guru, Chögyam Trungpa Rinpoche, in 1972. Lama Chimé encouraged her to work with Rinpoche, and it was with him that she ultimately made her most profound connection, studying with him from 1974 until his death in 1987. At the request of the Sixteenth Karmapa, she received the full bhikshuni ordination in the Chinese lineage of Buddhism in 1981 in Hong Kong. She served as the codirector of Karma Dzong in Boulder, Colorado, until moving in 1984 to rural Cape Breton, Nova Scotia, to be the director and now abbess of Gampo Abbey. Chögyam Trungpa Rinpoche gave her explicit instructions on establishing this monastery for Western monks and nuns.

Ani Pema currently teaches in the United States and Canada and plans for an increased amount of time in solitary retreat under the guidance of Venerable Dzigar Kongtrul Rinpoche. She is interested in helping to establish Tibetan Buddhist monasticism in the West. Her nonprofit, the Pema Chödrön Foundation, was set up to assist in this purpose, as well as to support Tibetan Buddhist nuns in India and Nepal and organizations that help at-risk individuals and populations in the United States and abroad.

She has written several books, including *How We Live Is How We Die, Welcoming the Unwelcome, The Wisdom of No Escape, Start Where You Are, When Things Fall Apart, The Places That Scare You, Becoming Bodhisattvas, Practicing Peace,* and *Living Beautifully.*